D1484947

Managing Your
Sales Team

Managing Your
Sales Team

*A practical guide to sales leadership
that will get the best results*

JOHN HUMPHRIES
2nd edition

How To Books

Published by How To Books Ltd, 3 Newtec Place,
Magdalen Road, Oxford OX4 1RE. United Kingdom.
Tel: (01865) 793806. Fax: (01865) 248780.
email: info@howtobooks.co.uk
http://www.howtobooks.co.uk

Second edition 1999

British Library Cataloguing in Publication Data.
A catalogue record for this book is available from
the British Library.

Editing by Alison Wilson
Cover design by Shireen Nathoo Design
Cover image PhotoDisc

Produced for How To Books by Deer Park Productions
Typeset by PDQ Typesetting, Stoke-on-Trent, Staffs.
Printed and bound by Cromwell Press, Trowbridge, Wiltshire

NOTE: The material contained in this book is set out in good
faith for general guidance and no liability can be accepted
for loss or expense incurred as a result of relying in particular
circumstances on statements made in the book. Laws and
regulations are complex and liable to change, and readers should
check the current position with the relevant authorities before
making personal arrangements.

Contents

List of Illustrations

Preface
to the 2nd edition

Having spent many years in sales management, it is my considered, but of course unbiased, opinion that managing sales is the most demanding of the management disciplines.

This is due to the fact that unlike the other management functions, the sales manager has to rely mainly upon just two resources for success: people and information. The people are not only the salespeople directly under the sales manager's control but also those in ancillary departments such as sales administration and marketing, together with production, finance and logistics. The necessary information refers to markets, customers, potential customers, products and competitive activity. Thus, in order to be successful, the sales manager must make the best possible use of these resources, particularly the people.

The main difficulty faced by most newly promoted sales managers is that they were promoted because they were good at selling. They now find themselves in the alien world of management and too often with no training for this new role. As a result they adopt the management style of their own manager, which may not be the best for their situation.

This book aims to help you cross this 'great divide' as quickly and painlessly as possible and to discover the pleasure and satisfaction that can come from managing and leading a happy and enthusiastic team to ever-growing success.

Each chapter deals with a specific aspect of sales management and is based on the experience I have been lucky enough to have acquired over many years, both as a sales manager and through advising a whole range of companies on their sales and marketing development. I have tried to answer some of the questions that sales managers often ask and each chapter concludes with exercises to help you think matters through. Suggested solutions to some of these can be found at the back of the book.

I hope you find this book useful in your aim to become a better sales manager. You will only know whether techniques work if you put them into practice. Good luck!

John Humphries

1

Identifying the Sales Manager's Role

The role of the sales manager is similar to that of other managers, namely to lead and motivate the team to achieve its objectives. The difference lies in the way in which the sales manager operates and uses his/her resources.

UNDERSTANDING THE RESPONSIBILITIES

Upon promotion, the sales manager will be given certain responsibilities. These are normally set out in the **job description** under such headings as Key Tasks, Principal Accountabilities or simply Main Responsibilities. These responsibilities could include:

- achieving agreed sales targets
- expanding the existing customer base
- recruiting sales staff
- training the staff
- preparing sales forecasts
- organising exhibitions.

In addition to those responsibilities identified in the job description, the sales manager is also responsible for the welfare of the team. Under this heading would be:

- motivating the team
- giving appropriate guidance and support
- developing individuals through coaching
- ensuring Health and Safety regulations are adhered to
- encouraging 'open' communication.

BECOMING ACCOUNTABLE

With responsibility comes accountability. The sales manager is ultimately accountable for any shortcomings in the team and the achievement of its objectives. In other words, this is where the buck stops. For example, the sales manager would have to give good reasons to senior management if the objectives have not been achieved.

ASSUMING AUTHORITY

This is the power or rights given to sales managers to enable them to fulfil their responsibilities. All authority has limits or parameters within which the sales manager is expected to operate such as:

- expenditure limits
- discounts to customers
- discipline of staff
- geographical boundaries.

It is important that you are fully aware of the extent of your authority, not only so that you do not exceed it, but also to enable you to operate to its limits.

ANALYSING YOUR ROLE

The role of the sales manager is wide and the main functions are:

1. **Planning** to reach the targets.
2. **Organising** your resources to meet the plan.
3. **Controlling** those resources to get the best use from them.
4. **Leading** your team in the most appropriate and effective manner.
5. **Recruiting** the right people for your team.
6. **Training** your staff to enable them to achieve their targets.
7. **Motivating** the individuals within your team.

Each of these functions is dealt with in detail in the following chapters.

DOING THE RIGHT THINGS

Here are a few tips which are particularly appropriate for the newly promoted or recruited sales manager:

- Learn how the team operates before suggesting any changes.
- Get to know your team as individuals. Everyone has a different personality. Talk to them to discover their strengths and weaknesses.

- Be flexible. Don't tie yourself to one style of management.
- Be prepared to learn from everyone, especially your team.
- Establish your position through co-operation and involvement.
- Earn the respect of your team by your actions.
- Attend a suitable training course.
- Practise what you have learned from this book.

AVOIDING MISTAKES

Everyone makes mistakes. The key is don't make the same one twice. By avoiding the following, you will give yourself a fighting chance:

- managing by threats or fear
- making changes before assessing the situation
- being influenced by how your predecessor managed the team
- appearing to be a know-all
- allowing yourself to be browbeaten by more experienced team members
- trying to be the best salesperson in your team
- setting yourself apart from your team.

CASE STUDY

Robert hears some home truths

There was a sales manager, whom we shall call Robert, who firmly believed that achieving the right results was the whole purpose of his being. He constantly harried, threatened and chivvied his salespeople to sell more and more. He never took their personal needs into consideration: he believed that if he could work twelve hours a day, his sales team should be able to do the same. He was immensely proud of the fact that he never missed a target. Therefore he was surprised when his sales director called him into his office.

'Robert, you really must make some changes in the way that you manage or we may have to dispense with your services,' began the director.

'But why?' Robert exploded. 'You know that I always make target!'

'That's true, but do you realise that you bring in between a quarter and a third of the business yourself each month?' the director asked.

'Well, that's because the salespeople are not pulling their weight,' Robert explained.

'As you spend more than half your time with customers, perhaps your team are not being managed correctly. Furthermore,' the sales director continued, 'the staff turnover in your department was almost one and a half times during the last twelve months. The cost of this constant recruitment almost offsets your sales revenue. I'm sure you agree that this is unacceptable. What do you suggest we do to improve things?'

'I don't know,' Robert said quietly.

'You could always attend a management training course. I have a list of possible courses here,' suggested the director. 'Look through the list and book yourself on one.'

It was with much reluctance that Robert attended a course but he had to admit that it helped to save his career and his job.

Unless the sales manager quickly realises that managing requires different skills from selling and that the art of good management is balancing the needs of the company with those of the team, then failure is staring him in the face.

QUESTIONS AND ANSWERS

Several of my team are better at selling than I am. This makes me feel inadequate. What can I do?

Remember that you are now a manager. Encourage them to sell and make sure you manage them correctly.

My predecessor was well liked by the team, who were sorry when he left. How can I live up to their expectations of me?

You are not your predecessor. Manage in the way you think is best. Ask your team what they liked about his style.

My company does not have a training policy. How can I persuade them to let me attend a sales managers' course?

Obtain details of suitable courses. Speak to your manager and present the benefits and cost effectiveness of you attending a course.

EXERCISES

1. List your main responsibilities and identify the authority you have for each.

2. Identify your current strengths and weaknesses as a sales manager. How will you develop the strengths and reduce the weaknesses?

3. You have recently joined a small engineering company as the sales manager. You have three sales engineers covering the whole country. Before your arrival, the managing director looked after the salespeople. Although you have been with the company for three months, he is still involved in the day-to-day sales activities, often countering your decisions and undermining your position with the sales team. What can you do to prevent his constant interference?

2

Planning

Planning is knowing where you want to go and working out the best way to get there with the resources available.

Planning is not a one-off activity, although it is true that strategic or long term planning is normally undertaken once a year, tactical planning is an on-going process.

PLANNING STRATEGICALLY

This begins with the **sales forecast** (see Chapter 9). Other factors need to be taken into account at this stage.

Planning by product

The majority of companies have a range of products or services to sell so begin by analysing each product. List the products or services and then rank them under:

(a) sales volume per annum
(b) profitability per unit (see Table 1).

Product	Sales volume per annum	Profitability per unit
A	2	5
B	4	1
C	3	3
D	1	6
E	5	4
F	6	2

Table 1.

From the above example we can see that products A and D have the highest sales volumes but the lowest profitability per unit, while product F has a low volume of sales but a high profitability. Therefore you can plan for more sales effort to be directed towards product F. Are A and D easier to sell? If so, why? How would a price increase affect the sales volumes of A and D?

Planning by customer

As with so many activities the 80/20 rule applies to sales. That is, about 80 per cent of the business comes from 20 per cent of the customers. This makes the company very vulnerable, for if just one of the 20 per cent goes out of business or transfers its allegiance to a competitor, a large proportion of sales revenue will be lost. One way to categorise the market is by the amounts that customers spend with you – for example, see Table 2.

Category	Average annual spend	No. of customers
A	£250,000 +	11
B	£100,000 +	28
C	£ 50,000 +	105
D	£ 25,000 +	220
E	£ 10,000 +	350
F	£ 2,000 +	450
G	0	500 est.

Table 2.

From Table 2 we can see that if we lose one customer from category A, we would need 2.5 Bs or 5 more Cs or 10 more Ds or 25 more Es to fill the gap.

While it is important to continue to service the most important customers, more time and effort needs to be spent on increasing the revenue of the middle order category customers and developing new ones.

Based upon the table, we would plan for the sales team to allocate its times as follows:

A – 20%
B – 15%
C
D } – 30%
E
F – 15%
G – 20% (it is vital to seek out new business)

With the above information, together with your sales forecast, you are now in a position to prepare your strategic sales plan. The plan should include known activities such as:

- major exhibitions
- promotional campaigns
- launch of new products/services.

PLANNING TACTICALLY

Tactical planning can be either reactive or proactive.

Reactive tactical planing is normally undertaken to counter unexpected or unplanned activities. These might include:

- Increased competitive activity – you could consider changing your discount strategy.
- Illness or departure of a team member – you will need to plan cover for that sales area.
- Increased costs of raw materials, transportation *etc* – can these be absorbed or will you have to replan your pricing policy?
- Change in the law affecting your products/services – this may require a rethink to your sales approach.
- Relocation of a major customer from one sales area to another – you will need to plan to deal with the effect this will have on the salespeople involved.

Proactive tactical planning is necessary to put in place events and activities not included in the strategic plan due to cost restraints, increased market information, changes in company policy and so on. These could include:

- local exhibitions
- formal training courses for you and/or your team
- mail shot campaign to boost sales of a declining product.

SETTING PERFORMANCE STANDARDS

People, particularly salespeople, need standards which they can work towards and by which they can judge their own performance.

Performance standards should always be quantifiable so that they can be easily compared with actual performance. When setting performance standards, it is essential that they are achievable, otherwise they will act as demovitators to those expected to reach them.

Setting sales targets

The setting of sales targets is one of the main bones of contention in any sales department. This is usually because targets are decided and presented to the team as a *fait accompli*.

Targets are based on sales forecasts. Too often these 'forecasts' are made by the board, who merely add a percentage to last year's figures and give it to the sales manager, who then divides the target by the number of people in the team and tells them what they have to achieve. The result is usually resistance, non commitment and demotivation.

Case study

A company manufacturing building materials required the sales team to produce a 25 per cent increase over last year's target. This was despite the fact that, although the team had tried very hard, owing to changes in the market they had missed the previous target by 15 per cent. The sales manager, who had not been involved in setting the new target, was faced with a demoralised team. What could he do? First of all he asked each representative to estimate their own targets. He compiled this information into a realistic sales forecast and attempted to present it to his board. They dismissed his forecast and told him to get on with achieving their figures. As a result, he resigned and took two of his best salespeople with him to a competitor.

The best way of setting targets is to:

- involve the team in setting them
- use the previous year's actual results
- obtain and use information about market changes, customer needs and competitive activity
- account for the abilities and experience of each salesperson
- set targets by product as well as overall revenue.

Targets must be realistic and achievable to gain the commitment of each and every member of the sales team.

Case study
The managing director of a small company producing health foods sought an increase in sales revenue of 15 per cent for the following year. The sales manager was not informed of this but was asked to make her own forecast. She involved her team of three in this exercise. These figures were accepted by the MD and she relayed this fact to her team who had committed themselves to achieving their targets. Despite making great efforts, the team just failed to reach their overall target figure. However, the managing director was not displeased as sales revenue had increased by 18.5 per cent.

Setting other performance standards
In addition to targets, performance standards can be set for other areas of sales activity such as:

- calls per day, week, month *etc*
- calls by customer category
- time spent per call by customer category
- products by volume
- cost per call (travel, time, entertaining *etc*)
- discounting.

However, when setting such standards, remember to:

(a) Tell the team why standards have been set and how they will benefit.
(b) Involve the team in setting them.

SETTING BEHAVIOURAL STANDARDS

Behavioural standards, although difficult to quantify, are just as important as performance standards.

Personal appearance
Although the current trend with many companies is to 'dumb down' the dress code and do away with the formal business approach in favour of 'smart casual', this is rarely appropriate for salespeople. The first thing that the customer or prospect notices about the sales representative is his or her appearance. If this is not acceptable to the customer, the salesperson has to try and overcome this negative

attitude of the customer, without knowing the reason why.

As a rule of thumb, the salespeople should dress in a manner acceptable to the majority of the market they are servicing. For example, the 'business suit' is the norm for the IT, financial and general commercial areas. This can be relaxed slightly for FMCG (Fast Moving Consumer Goods), while the farming community prefer a more 'country' approach. Modern fashionable clothes are ideal for the 'younger' industries such as fashion, music, entertainment and haircare.

Therefore you need to set dress standards according to your market. It goes without saying that all salespeople should be clean and tidy.

The car

The majority of sales representatives have a company car to enable them to perform their sales functions. It is essential that the car is kept clean both inside and out and is well maintained for obvious reasons. You can set quantifiable standards such as washing the car once a week and having it serviced at predetermined intervals. If, however, it is the company's policy for the sales team to provide their own vehicles, then it is more difficult to insist on these standards.

Equipment

This would include presentation materials, samples, order forms, report forms and so on. The standard would be to ensure that the salespeople have sufficient supplies in presentable condition.

Administration

Paperwork is the bane of every salesperson's life but it is something that must be done. You will need to set standards regarding both accuracy and timing. For example, weekly reports must be completed and with you by the following Monday. Today, much of this administration can be done on a lap top or PC, making it much easier to compile and transmit.

Maintaining contact

As salespeople should be away from the office for most of the working week and it is not always possible for the sales manager to have daily face-to-face contact with them, some form of contact system needs to be employed. This may be by telephone each day or less regularly if appropriate. Mobile phones make it easier to keep in touch these days.

In addition to the above, you may decide to set standards on time keeping, co-operation, attitude, communication skills *etc*. However, it is worth bearing in mind that the more draconian you appear to be, the less likelihood there is of the standards being reached or maintained.

QUESTIONS AND ANSWERS

How can I get my team to supply the information I need to enable me to plan strategically?

Decide what information you need. Explain the importance of this to your team and how it will help them by making targets achievable.

Traditionally targets have been given to me by my sales director and I am expected to implement them even though they are virtually impossible to achieve. How can I influence my director?

Prepare your plan and present it to the director before he gives you his targets. Explain the reasons for and benefits of your plan.

I want to introduce behavioural standards to my team. How should I go about this?

Initially keep to just two or three standards and introduce them to your team at a meeting, giving them the reasons for the standards together with the benefits.

EXERCISES

1. List those performances and behaviours for which you could set standards to benefit your team.

2. Brian has recently been promoted to area sales manager and has been asked to prepare a sales plan for the coming year. What information and source documents could be use for this?

3. Why are behavioural standards important?

3

Organising and Controlling Your Team

ORGANISING YOUR SALES TEAM

Having prepared your strategic sales plan, you now need to utilise your most valuable resource, people, to put the plan into action in the most effective way to achieve your objectives. This is a matter of deciding who sells what to whom.

How you organise your team will largely depend upon:

(a) the product range
(b) the types of customers
(c) the experience of your salespeople.

It can be done in one or a combination of the following ways:

By geographical area

Each salesperson is allocated an area and sells the full range of products or services to all types of customers. This is particularly suitable where the products are non technical and the customers are of a similar type. For example: books and home improvements.

The advantages of this system are that only one representative will visit each customer and the area is confined to one person, thus being cost effective in terms of travelling. The disadvantage is the difficulty in dividing the territories so that they are fair to each salesperson and giving them an equal opportunity to reach their targets. As a result some geographical areas will be comparatively small, such as London or Merseyside, while others may include the whole of Scotland or Wales. Geographical areas may have to be adjusted each year depending upon the results achieved and relocation of customers.

By product

If the range of products includes some which require more expertise than others or require different selling skills, each representative can be given specific products to sell depending upon the individual's experience. An example might be a software company where one group of salespeople sells 'off the shelf' programs, while others sell bespoke packages.

An advantage with this method is that it provides a career path for promotion within the sales team. Disadvantages are that more than one representative may visit some customers and more travelling would be involved as the areas would be larger, which may make it less cost effective.

By customer

This is the method often used by FMCG companies. One group of sales representatives would sell to independent retail outlets on a geographical basis, while another group, often referred to as national account executives, would sell to the larger customers such as wholesalers and supermarket chains where negotiation skills are more important.

The advantages and disadvantages are similar to that for selling by product.

By market segment

Where a company manufactures products which are sold to different types of industries, each representative concentrates on one specific industry and thus gains vital experience in that particular field. For example: a company manufacturing bearings sells to the marine industry, the automotive industry, railways and general engineering. Each of the representatives specialises in one industry type.

Again the disadvantage is the geographical distribution of the customers resulting in much time spent travelling. However, this is usually outweighed by the expertise and market information that the salesperson gains.

Only you can decide which is the most appropriate system for you. Don't be afraid to experiment and make changes.

ORGANISING THE TERRITORIES

Travelling is the biggest time waster in sales. Where possible, your salespeople should live in or very close to the area which they are servicing, which will help to reduce this wasted time.

Many sales representatives will visit their customers on a regular basis, particularly when seeking repeat business from the retail trade. It is sensible therefore to organise **journey plans**.

This can be done by grouping customers geographically and planning daily routes with the aid of a road map.

Where customers require different frequency of visits, group them into weekly, monthly or quarterly visits and again by using a map, regular routes can be planned.

Where customers are widely scattered, more care needs to be taken when planning visits. If a representative based in Bristol has to call on a customer in Newcastle, make sure that the visit is really necessary and if it is, try to arrange to see other customers en route.

Case study

Ron was the sales manager for a firm of specialist printers and signwriters which had its head office in Swindon. He was responsible for four salesmen who lived near Cardiff, Birmingham, Liverpool and Edinburgh respectively. Each had a number of regular customers to service and were actively encouraged to seek new business for which there was a handsome financial incentive. Ron assumed (always a very dangerous thing to do) that the salesmen would look for business within their undefined geographical areas. However, it soon transpired that the salesman from Cardiff was seeing prospects in the Midlands, the man based in Scotland was travelling to Manchester and the Birmingham salesman was going to London, for which Ron was responsible. This was not only costly in travel and time but led to the salesmen accusing one another of encroachment and cherry picking.

Ron had no option but to gather his team together and organise defined territories. Although this caused some initial discontent because the salesmen were losing customers that they had acquired from other areas, they did gain customers from their colleagues.

Salespeople being naturally keen and competitive will go anywhere for business unless they are organised, which, as the sales manager, is your responsibility.

CONTROLLING YOUR SALES TEAM

In the context of sales management, controlling should be synonymous with the word **monitoring**.

Controlling is a matter of comparing actual performance with the standards set and taking the necessary action to rectify any negative variances.

Controlling performance standards

As previously mentioned, these should be quantifiable so that actual performance can be easily measured against the standards.

The frequency of controls will depend upon the standard being measured. They should not happen so often that the salespeople feel that their every action is being checked, but at the same time they need to be frequent enough to enable any required action to be taken before it is too late.

Targets set annually still need to be monitored on a weekly, monthly or quarterly basis, depending upon the products and market. If you leave it until the end of the year, it is obviously too late to make amendments.

In order to monitor performance, you will need data, which would normally be supplied by the salespeople, in the form of orders, reports and returns. Therefore you have to rely upon the honesty of the team. This should be no problem provided you have earned their trust and respect. There may be the odd occasion when some of the information you receive from this source strikes you as suspicious: for example, a call rate which is much higher than the team average. In such cases, talk face-to-face to the individual concerned to establish the facts before taking any action or jumping to conclusions.

Before taking action to rectify negative variances, consider carefully all possible reasons for the discrepancy. There may be very valid ones such as illness or holidays. Also look for a trend. If one of your team has not met target one week, leave it for the next two or three weeks and then if that person is consistently below target, take action, which initially should be a discussion with that individual to discover the facts and resolve the matter mutually.

Case study

Daphne was given the task of managing six salespeople to sell batteries to the independent retail market. This was a new project and so the team had to find and establish their own customers. Each was given a geographical territory and Daphne set a call rate standard of ten calls per day. After a month had passed, Daphne learned that the average call rate was only seven per day. She called her team together and berated them for not reaching the standard. She was not prepared to listen to excuses or reasons. A month later the call rate was up to standard but the sales revenue had hardly increased. Once again she called a meeting to criticise the team's performance.

'Do you want quality or quantity?' asked one of the salespeople.
'Both.' she replied.

'In that case may I suggest that you come out with each of us to
see what life is really like out there?'

Reluctantly, Daphne agreed. After spending a day out with each
of her team, she realised that she had set her standards too high and
modified them accordingly.

That is why it is so important to involve the team when setting
standards.

Keeping records

In order to control effectively, you will need to record actual
performances to detect trends and changes.

Table 3 shows an example of a call rate record.

Weekly call rate							
Name	Standard set	Actual performance					
		1	2	3	4	5	6
J Smith	25	22	25	20	26	23	25
B Green	20	18	16	20	19	20	21
D Brown	20	15	16	15	14	12	16
E White	20	20	20	19	22	21	20
L Black	18	13	15	15	17	18	18

Table 3.

You may decide to set different standards for each individual
depending upon such factors as their experience, size of territory
and customer type. As can be seen from this example, D Brown is well
below the standard, thus requiring some action on your part. L Black
started slowly but is building up to the standard set.

Controlling behavioural standards

Being subjective, these standards will require you to make judgements
to compare actual with standard. You will only be in a position to
make comparisons when you are with the salesperson concerned. The

simplest method is to use a form and rate each item on a 1 to 4 basis, 1 being to the required standard and 4 well below (see Table 4).

Name...			
Appearance	1	2	3	4
Car: outside	1	2	3	4
inside	1	2	3	4
Presentation	1	2	3	4
material	1	2	3	4
Attitude	1	2	3	4
Time keeping	1	2	3	4
Route planning	1	2	3	4
Communication skills	1	2	3	4

Table 4.

The main point to remember when assessing these standards is to be fair to everyone and judge people against the standards and not against each other. Figures 1, 2 and 3 show examples of other reports that you may wish to use to adapt for controlling your team.

QUESTIONS AND ANSWERS

One of my sales representatives lives in her area which covers Greater Manchester and Merseyside. Her husband has recently been promoted by his company and this will mean that they have to relocate to Bristol. I want to keep her with my team, so what can I do?

Unless it is a condition of service that all representatives live on their territory, you could not dismiss her on these grounds, even if you wished to. This may give you the opportunity to reorganise the sales areas in order to accommodate her in the Bristol area. If this is not possible, explain the situation to her, emphasising that she will have a long drive to reach her customers. Are you able to bear the additional travel costs? Will you pay for her to stay in hotels during the week? Calculate the additional sales revenue required to meet these additional costs. Discuss the matter with the sales team, they may have an acceptable solution.

WEEKLY REPORT (1)

Week commencing: 3rd May 19XX   **Name**: Brian Greenway

Date	Name of Company	Cat.	Order Value	Product Type	Comments
3 May	Tomlinson & Co	C			Will order next month
3 May	G. D. Wallis	B	£1,250	t43	Deliver a.s.a.p.
3 May	Brown & White	C	£500	m7	Using competition
4 May	Wickstead Ltd	F			No requirements
4 May	Belford & Sons	C	£1,000	t43	
4 May	Dickson & Black Ltd	F	£450	s5	New customer

Fig. 1. Weekly sales report (1).

WEEKLY REPORT (2)

Week beginning: 5th July 19XX

NAME: Susan Watkins

Date	Company	Contact name	Initial visit	Surv	Dem	Order received	Order value
5 July	Billings & Co	Tom Smith		/			(£12,500 approx)
5 July	Lillistones	G Wilson	/				
6 July	Dicksons	J Morris			/	/	£18,750
6 July	Milford Ltd	L Thompson	/				
7 July	Roberts & Co	D Roberts			/		(£15,000 approx)
7 July	D Philpots Ltd	H Peters				/	£22,600

Fig. 2. Weekly sales report (2)

WEEKLY ANALYSIS

Week No: 23

Name	Visits by customer category							Sales by product type				
	A	B	C	D	E	F	TOT	L4	M23	T6	H15	B9
David	5	10	26	12	7	0	60	0	3	9	1	11
Jane	3	7	21	15	19	7	72	2	4	14	3	12
Peter	8	14	15	18	10	2	67	1	7	10	0	16
Susan	2	7	17	16	19	14	75	3	8	9	2	21
Tony	10	16	21	7	0	0	54	4	2	8	0	14
Totals	28	54	100	68	55	23	328	10	24	50	6	73

So what does this tell us?

Generally – Too much attention is given to customers in the C and D categories and insufficient to F (prospects). Sales appear to be concentrated on products B9 and T6, we need to sell more L4s and H15s. What could be the reasons for this?

David – Spend less time on C customers and more time visiting prospects. Needs to improve his sales of L4s and H15s.

Jane – Good spread of visits and product range sold.

Peter – Too much time with A customers and not enough with F. Concentrating on products T6 and B9 to the detriment of the others.

Susan – Good ratio of visits but needs to spread the product range sold.

Tony – Must spend more time with E and F customers. Time spent with A group is not reflected in the sales.

Fig. 3. Weekly sales analysis.

One of my salesmen constantly falls below the acceptable behavioural standards: his car is always messy, he is late for sales meetings and he does not always conform to the dress code. Yet he is good at his job and always meets his performance standards. What should I do?

Talk to him. Explain the situation and the problem it causes you and the effect it may have on his colleagues. Sometimes performance standards have to take precedence over behavioural ones.

EXERCISES

1. How are your sales areas organised at present? Is this the most effective method? What improvements could you make?

2. Design control systems which are simple to use and provide you with the required information.

3. Mike has been with you for four years. Until three months ago, he was one of your star performers. However, recently his sales figures have fallen well below target and he has become sloppy with his paperwork. What might be the reason for this? What can you do to bring him back to scratch?

4

Leading Your Team

LEADERSHIP AS A MANAGEMENT SKILL

It is a common fallacy that to lead a sales team successfully you have to be the best salesperson. Whilst it helps to possess good selling skills in order to gain credibility, it is far more important to have the ability to lead the team to success. Having said that, there are of course many small sales teams consisting of a sales manager and just one or two sales executives, and the manager must do his or her share of selling. In these cases, the manager needs to allocate time carefully between selling and managing.

Leaders require different skills for different situations. For example, some people make excellent leaders in times of war, *eg* Sir Winston Churchill, but are less successful in peacetime. Similarly, there are people who are first class leaders in the armed forces but are unsuccessful at leading business teams. As with so many things, leadership is a matter of horses for courses.

Determining your leadership/management style

By completing the following inventory you will obtain some insights into your leadership style, how appropriate it is and how it may be affecting others. Below are ten aspects of management, each consisting of five statements. Select the statement that most reflects your own thinking and give it a rating of 4. Then choose the next most representative statement and give it 3 points and do likewise with the remaining statements in each set.

The ratings are:

4 – Most representative; I agree strongly.
3 – The next most representative.
2 – Next most representative.
1 – Next to least representative.
0 – Least representative.

Do not change any of your ratings; your first answer is usually the most accurate. When you have completed the inventory enter your points on the scoring grid.

---

1. Role perception

....(a) I see my work group as a team in which I function as a member, bringing resources that they need to achieve their goals.

....(b) One of my priority roles as a manager is to see that my people are happy in their work, since good morale is the key to success.

....(c) My style is to spell out the details of the assignment as clearly as possible, then step back and let the team get on with it.

....(d) When the needs of my team and the organisation are in conflict, my role is to find a compromise solution that satisfies both sides.

....(e) I avoid a democratic style of management because it leads to poor decisions and reduced productivity from people who lack the necessary experience and resources.

2. View of authority

....(a) I regard authority, not compromise or consultation, as the prime tool of management and the ultimate source of a manager's power.

....(b) When I make a decision, I outline the reasons behind it so that my team will see the logic and accept it.

....(c) I'm pretty good at integrating our goals and standards with the skills and abilities of my people.

....(d) I rely on precedent and past decisions, since these are the major sources of my authority.

....(e) Sometimes the expectations and standards that come down from above are arbitrary and rigid, and I have to protect my team from them.

3. Setting goals and standards

....(a) On many matters my hands are tied and I act in accordance with our policies, procedures and precedent.

....(b) I like my people to 'buy in' to the goals and activities that I set for them and to feel that the ideas are theirs.

....(c) Close supervision is important in setting the pace, standard and the importance of the work at hand.

....(d) I avoid imposing my will on my team; they work out their own goals and do their own planning.

....(e) The key to high productivity is to help my team to develop a personal commitment to goals and standards that become theirs through involvement and planning.

4. View of work and people

....(a) I sometimes have to serve as a 'buffer zone' between the needs of my team and the policies and procedures of the company.

....(b) The work that I supervise is not inherently enjoyable or challenging, and a system of close control is necessary to keep people productive.

....(c) Each of my team brings special resources and talents to the job, and I encourage them to arrange assignments so as to draw on each others' strengths.

....(d) People usually go along with the assignments I make, but this requires a flexible style of management on my part.

....(e) In today's business climate, there is relatively little latitude for independent action; our roles are well defined.

5. Planning and work scheduling

....(a) It's important to me that my team are involved in planning the work they perform.

....(b) Many of the decisions I make are actually determined by well established policies or by the authorisation of my superiors.

....(c) Whilst I must exercise control over situations, I try to get the opinions and inputs of my people and utilise them when appropriate.

....(d) Managers who involve their staff in making decisions and setting goals are abdicating a major responsibility and inviting problems.

....(e) Strong discipline and difficult goals set by upper management only serve to frustrate people and their managers.

6. Giving feedback

....(a) I like to reward successes in group settings and address failures in private with just the two of us.

....(b) One of the reasons my people think of me as a friend is that I avoid correcting them or causing them discomfort.

....(c) I avoid becoming personally involved in giving employee feedback; they don't like appraisals and neither do I.

....(d) I like to see my team giving feedback to one another on each other's performance.

....(e) When I give criticism, people often don't know how to take it; they become defensive and offer excuses.

7. Team building

....(a) My people expect me to make assignments, plan their work and evaluate them. Overseeing their work is my job.

....(b) I get my people to plan their work and their goals so as to achieve our company's mission and our personal growth needs at the same time.

....(c) As a manager, I know my people and their limitations fairly well and can give assignments that are appropriate to their capabilities.

....(d) I let my people handle the work; they know where to find me when they need me.

....(e) I prefer a consultative role, supplying ideas and getting my team to 'massage them' until they become their own.

8. Implementation

....(a) I follow a policy of 'management by exception', paying less attention to the normal flow of 'business as usual' work.

....(b) I am 'on call' to my people to help them to fight fires when necessary or when plans or goals need to be revised.

....(c) I expect strict and speedy execution from my people, who know that I run a 'tight ship'.

....(d) I provide relatively little direction, preferring to function as a support person who creates a climate of high worker satisfaction.

....(e) The quality of my group's output is enhanced by encouraging their increased participation in setting goals and planning of implementation.

9. Evaluation

....(a) I tend to avoid discussing my people's mistakes or failures with them, since people benefit more from encouragement and a pat on the back.

....(b) I try to avoid subjective evaluations of my team's performance and favour the objectivity of checklists and formal appraisals.

....(c) I view evaluations as a learning experience for manager and employee alike and part of every project we undertake.

....(d) In our daily interactions, I give feedback to my people frequently and informally. This is preferable to formal evaluation sessions.

....(e) In my opinion most people do not like to be evaluated.

10. Management philosophy

....(a) I believe that people who are going to be directly affected by a decision should participate in making it.

....(b) I'm convinced most people would rather not take on more responsibility or authority. They look to management to plan, direct and control.

....(c) It's important that my people accept and like me; managers who are not liked by their people are usually less effective.

....(d) Although my door is always open to my people, I usually have minimum participation in their work unless a crisis occurs.

....(e) With people less and less interested in their work, we managers are hard pressed to get high productivity from them.

Scoring Grid

1		2		3		4		5	
A	T	A	H	A	I	A	S	A	T
B	S	B	M	B	M	B	H	B	I
C	I	C	T	C	H	C	T	C	M
D	M	D	I	D	S	D	M	D	H
E	H	E	S	E	T	E	I	E	S

6		7		8		9		10	
A	M	A	H	A	I	A	S	A	T
B	S	B	T	B	M	B	I	B	H
C	I	C	S	C	H	C	T	C	S
D	T	D	I	D	S	D	M	D	M
E	H	E	M	E	T	E	H	E	I

When you have transferred all your ratings from the statements, add up the totals for each group. The group letters are shown to the right of each box.

Sum of 10 T boxes ....
Sum of 10 S boxes.........
Sum of 10 H boxes........
Sum of 10 M boxes ....
Sum of 10 I boxes ....

The grid in Figure 4 (page 40) is based on Blake and Mouton's Managerial Grid. It illustrates each style in relation to its concern with the task and concern for people. There is also a brief description of how other people may perceive each style.

Is your style appropriate?

Your highest score on the above inventory indicates your 'preferred' style of leadership, that is the style in which you feel most comfortable when operating. With the exception of the ineffective style, no style is necessarily right or wrong, better or worse. That will depend upon the situation and the people concerned.

The questions that you should ask yourself are:

● Is my preferred style appropriate for most of the situations in which I find myself?

● How does my preferred style affect other people, particularly those I am trying to lead?

One of the main skills required of a leader in business is flexibility: being able to change the style to suit the situation or people.

CHOOSING THE RIGHT LEADERSHIP STYLE

As a sales manager, there may be times when you will need to change your style to be most effective. Let's consider some situations.

Hard   This style is particularly appropriate in emergency situations such as getting employees out of a burning building. It can also be effective in the short term to

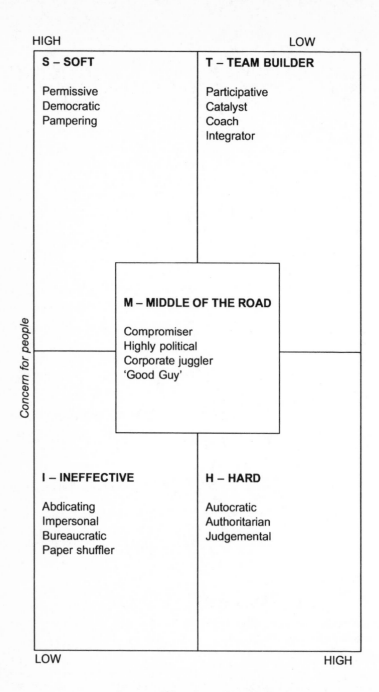

Concern with tasks and production
Fig. 4. Blake and Mouton's Managerial Grid.

accomplish an unusual, one-time, extraordinary effort, for example running a special promotion to get lagging sales up by the end of the quarter.

Soft   Can be useful when dealing with new, inexperienced salespeople or others who require a nurturing approach to improve their confidence.

Middle   Can be effective if you have sound judgement and enough charisma and personality to get your team to trust you. May be used when passing on unpleasant news or tasks from above. However, beware, as this style can be seen as manipulative.

Team builder Probably the ideal style for a sales manager as it shows high concern for both people and the task and you will find few situations where this style is not appropriate.

Remember, you cannot force others to accept your preferred style; it is up to you to adapt.

Factors affecting your style

Unfortunately we do not live in an ideal world and many factors may affect the style you use. These are some of them:

Organisational structure
As companies become more complex, managers must learn how to negotiate, compromise, adapt and accommodate.

Nature of work
Some tasks are pleasant; others less so. Some working environments make managing easy; others less so.

Culture and climate
The philosophy of the organisation, its norms and culture, climate and tempo, all exert their influences on how you manage and lead.

Degree of pressure
Given time you can invest in the coaching and development of your team. But under pressure for immediate results, you are pushed towards a hard or task-oriented style.

Expectations of your team
You must respond to the needs and values of your team.

Relationships upwards
How you are led from above will shape the way you behave in return.

Relationships downwards
The trust and openness of downward communications will influence your leadership style.

Personality
Your genes and upbringing have made it easier for you to behave in some ways than in others.

QUESTIONS AND ANSWERS

How do I know what styles are most appropriate?

Try different ones and observe the results.

I operate a team building style with my sales staff which is effective. However, my manager's preferred style is hard. He tries to exercise the style over my team at every opportunity. This is undermining their confidence. How can I prevent this from happening?

You will have to discuss the matter with your manager and explain the negative effect he is having on your team.

If my preferred style is opposite to that which is expected of me, am I in the wrong job?

If this dichotomy is proving to be too stressful and you are unable to alter it, then the answer must be yes.

EXERCISES

1. List situations which occur regularly in your job and decide which leadership style you should adopt for each.

2. Analyse the preferred style of your manager. If it is unacceptable to you, how can you get your manager to be more flexible?

3. Alec Taylor is the sales manager for Grimshaw Ltd, an engineering company which is part of T. R. Holdings plc. Another company in the group has closed down and three of its sales representatives have been transferred to Grimshaws. These sales people have been told to report to Alec Taylor's office at 9.00am on Monday. They are kept waiting for 20 minutes before Alec arrives and sits behind his desk.

'Well gentlemen, you are working for Grimshaws now, a very different kettle of fish from your last company. I'm not surprised it closed. I can assure you that you will have to work to earn your money here. You will be expected to make 30 calls a week. We have a sales meeting every Friday at 5.30pm, everyone will attend and no excuses are accepted. You will telephone me between six and seven every evening and report on your day's activities. I expect your weekly reports on my desk by 9.00am every Monday. These reports will be complete, accurate and neatly written. Richard Wilson will give you details of your territories and customer records. Right, any questions?'

'The products are quite different from those we have been dealing with,' said one of the salespeople. 'So do we get any training?'

'Training?' replied Taylor with astonishment. 'You're supposed to be experienced salespeople aren't you? You'll pick it up as you go along.'

With that, the three sales reps trooped back into the sales office.

(a) What style of management does Alec Taylor practise?
(b) How many statements can you discover to substantiate your assessment?
(c) How would you describe the likely morale of the team?
(d) What problems do you think Alec Taylor has in staffing his department and what can you suggest to improve the situation?
(e) What do you think will be the likely effect on the long-term performance on Grimshaws?

5

Recruiting Your Team

THE NEED FOR RECRUITMENT

There are two reasons for recruiting salespeople, either because one of the existing team has left, for whatever reason, or because you are increasing the number of people in the team. In both cases, the principles of good recruiting and selecting are the same.

THE RIGHT JOB AND THE RIGHT PERSON

The job description

It is essential to qualify the parameters of the job. A **job description** is a document which sets down the duties and responsibilities of the job holder. It relates purely to the job and not to the person. If a job description already exists, this is the time to update it or rewrite it if necessary. If there is no formal job description, then one should be compiled before beginning the recruitment process.

The main purpose of the job description is to provide both employee and employer with a shared understanding of the job. It is also a useful document for recruitment and staff appraisal.

While job descriptions will vary in format from company to company, they should all contain the following information.

- **Job title** – *ie* the title used within the company, which could be Sales Representative, Sales Executive, Area Sales Manager and so on.

- **Reporting line** – the title to which the job holder reports and the titles of any jobs reporting to the job holder. This may also take the form of an organisation chart.

- **Purpose of job** – a single sentence defining the reason for the existence of the job, *eg* for a sales person it might be 'To sell the company's products profitably to achieve agreed targets'.

- **Key tasks** – this is a list of the major duties and responsibilities of the job holder, *eg* 'To maintain regular contact with existing customers'.

- **Additional responsibilities** – more detailed description such as 'attend sales meetings'; 'ensure that the car is clean and presentable'.

Figure 5 is an example of a simple job description.

It is essential that job descriptions are kept up to date to reflect the current demands of the job.

Who is the right person for the job?

Having defined the job, your next task is to decide on the right person to fill it. This is best done by completing an **Employee Profile**, a description of the ideal employee under specific headings such as:

- **Age range** — May be useful for compatibility with existing team and customer expectation. Beware of being too restrictive.

- **Appearance** — Subjective judgement related to the environment.

- **Experience** — Previous work experience necessary to carry out the job. Decide which is more important, sales or industry experience.

- **Qualifications** — Academic and professional qualifications. Do not request over-qualified people.

- **Skills** — Essential skills such as driving, typing, photography and so on.

- **Health** — That which is necessary to perform the job.

- **Location** — May be necessary to specify accessibility or local knowledge.

As it is unlikely that you will attract someone who fits your ideal profile in every category, the profile should contain two columns: ideal and acceptable. An employee profile for the above job may look as shown in Figure 6.

JOB DESCRIPTION

JOB TITLE: Senior Sales Executive

REPORT TO: Sales Manager

PURPOSE: Achieve or exceed agreed sales targets for the company's range of feedstuffs and fertilizers within the assigned geographical area.

KEY TASKS:

1. Obtain orders which meet or exceed established targets.

2. Arrange visits to existing customers to ensure maximum coverage of the territory.

3. Arrange visits to other farmers, horticulturalists and nurserymen in the area to promote the company's products.

4. Provide product related, technical assistance to customers.

5. Obtain and communicate to the sales manager information relating to the market and competitors.

ADDITIONAL RESPONSIBILITIES:

1. Attend shows and exhibitions as required.

2. Complete all necessary administration on time.

3. Ensure that the car is clean and mechanically maintained.

4. Carry an adequate supply of company literature and samples.

5. Attend sales meetings as requested.

6. Assist other sales executives as necessary.

Fig. 5. A job description.

EMPLOYEE PROFILE

Category	Ideal	Acceptable
Age range	35 – 50	30 – 55
Appearance	Mature, smart, clean	Appropriate
Experience	5 yrs sales in farming or horticulture	5 yrs sales in similar industry
Qualifications	'O' level English, Maths, Biology or GCSE equivalent	'O' level English, Maths, or GCSE equivalent
Skills	Clean driving licence, practical farming skills	Clean driving licence
Health	Fully mobile	Fully mobile
Location	Devon/Cornwall	S.W. England

Fig. 6. A employee profile.

The purposes of the Employee Profile are to:

- prepare the advertisement copy
- assess applications
- assist in the preparation of the interview.

ATTRACTING THE RIGHT PEOPLE

There are various ways of bringing job vacancies to the attention of prospective employees. The most appropriate for salespeople are:

- Company notice board/newsletter — there may be suitable people within the company; advertise as you would in the press (see below).

- Recruitment agencies — a number of agencies specialise in sales-people; their fees normally amount to three to six months of the salary offered; the agency may not always carefully vet the people they recommend.

- Recruitment consultancies — provide a more detailed service than agencies; they may prepare the employee profile, advertise and undertake initial interviews, offering you three or four candidates for final selection; their fees are higher.

- Press advertising — the most popular method for recruiting sales-people.
  - National press — can be expensive; is it necessary to advertise nationally for a job in Scotland?
  - Provincial press — less expensive; useful if the job is localised.
  - Local press — ideal for tele-sales and similar positions.
  - Trade press — very suitable when you want people with industry experience, eg *Farmers Weekly* for the above job.

How to design a recruitment advertisement

The objective of the advertisement is to sell the vacancy to the right people, in competition with tens, even hundreds of other advertisements. Therefore the advertising copy must attract 'AIDA', in other words:

ATTENTION

Media – advertise in the most appropriate media, *ie* those that the right people are likely to read.

Size – the larger the advertisement, the more chance of it attracting attention; make it as large as you can afford.

Position – the top of the right hand page, if possible.

Headline – should be eye catching but not gimmicky.

INTEREST

Job – the job title.

Rewards – salary, car and the financial incentives; avoid such terms as OTE £30,000, experienced sales people will not be impressed.

Person – a précis of the employee profile.

Location – where the job is situated.

DESIRE

Give readers the desire to respond by expanding the above, and including other relevant information such as training, promotional prospects and so on.

ACTION

How to apply – names, address, telephone number and method of application (see below).

The success of a recruitment advertisement is judged on whether or not the right person was recruited, not on the number of replies.

How should a salesperson be asked to reply to an advertisement?

The method of applying will provide the reader with an indication of the **culture** of the company. Most salespeople will respond favourably to the informal approach such as, 'Phone Bob Green, Sales Manager on (telephone number) between 10.00am and 4.00pm today or tomorrow, for an informal discussion'. If readers are asked to 'Write to the Personnel Department for an application form', it will indicate an impersonal culture; the response from potential sales employees is likely to be low. If you ask people to send their CV do not respond by sending them an application form. They will either tear it up or return it with an appropriate 'comment'.

The advantage of asking people to telephone you is that you will be able to make an initial assessment of their suitability from their voice and how they answer your questions. Questions should be non-

SENIOR SALES EXECUTIVE

SALARY £21,000 + COMMISSION + CAR
DEVON & CORNWALL

JOB
To sell the company's range of feedstuffs and fertilizers to farmers, horticulturalists and nurserymen in the S.W. of England.

Visiting both existing customers and seeking new, viable business.

Full product training will be provided.

This is a key position in a team of six sales people.

PERSON
Applicants should have at least 5 years' selling experience preferably in the agricultural industry. Knowledge of farming will be an advantage.

Must be numerate and of smart appearance.

Preferred age range 35 – 50.

COMPANY
Based in Bristol, this family run company has served the industry for the past 75 years, producing a comprehensive range of feedstuffs and fertilizers.

TO APPLY
Telephone Bob Green, Sales Manager on 321 45678 between 10.30am and 4.00pm on 17th/18th/19th May 200X for informal discussion, or send C.V. if preferred.

W. DODDS & SONS LTD., CARLTON MILLS, KEYNSHAM, BRISTOL BS6 2XZ

Fig. 7. Advertisement for a sales vacancy.

aggressive but seek information, such as:

- name and address
- previous work experience
- what prompted them to respond.

From this information you can decide whether to invite them for interview, send them an application form or thank them for contacting you.

Designing application forms

These are normally produced by the company and are designed to cover all employee positions within the company. Many of these ask for too much detail. Do you really want to know the maiden name of the applicant's mother or details of their primary education? Others are very out of date. I came across one recently which still asked for details of the applicant's service with HM Forces.

Application forms should encompass the categories on the employee profile. If the company form is unsuitable, design your own. An example is shown in Figure 8.

HOLDING JOB INTERVIEWS

Which applicants should you interview?

Compare the written application with the employee profile and invite for an interview those candidates which fit it most closely. In most cases, six to eight interviews should be sufficient for a sales position. Always write to the unsuccessful people, thanking them for their application. This is a common courtesy, too often ignored by employers, which will reflect well on you and your organisation.

Always telephone the people that you wish to interview to arrange a mutually convenient appointment. This will show that you are a caring person who understands that candidates will not necessarily be able to drop everything to attend at your bidding.

Planning the interview

Read each application form or CV carefully and decide what additional information you wish to obtain at the interview. Plan the format of the interview as follows:

- Introduction to relax the interviewee.

APPLICATION FORM

NAME:

ADDRESS:

TEL NO:

QUALIFICATIONS:
  ACADEMIC:

  PROFESSIONAL:

WORK EXPERIENCE – Please give details of last three jobs
                    or ten years' work, whichever is longer.

Company Name & Address   *Position*   *Responsibilities*

HOBBIES & INTERESTS:

Signature:_____   Date:_____

Use the reverse of this form to write any other details you wish to provide.

Fig. 8. Job application form.

- Obtain relevant information from the candidate.

- Explain the job and give details of the company.

- Tell the candidate when you will be making a decision.

How long should an interview take? This will depend upon the seniority of the post and the complexity of the job. However, for most sales positions, 45 minutes to 1 hour should be sufficient if you propose to make a decision after single interviews. Should you decide to hold second interviews for a shortlist of three candidates, then 30 minutes will be enough for the initial interview. Always allow yourself at least 30 minutes between interviews to make notes about the last interviews and prepare yourself for the next.

Conducting the interview
1. Introduction
This should include a welcoming statement, introduction of yourself and tell the interviewee the form that the interview will take.

Example: 'Good morning Mr White, thank you for coming to see me. My name is Bob Green and I am the sales manager with whom you would be working. Please take a seat. During the interview, which will take about 45 minutes, I would like you to tell me more about yourself and your working experience, then I will tell you more about the job and the company and finally what the next stage will be. If you have any questions then please don't hesitate to ask me. Is that OK?'

2. Obtaining information
You will only gain information by asking questions. However, you will not relax the candidate by asking too many at the beginning. An ideal opening question would be: 'Tell me about your work experience since you joined Wilson & Co four years ago'. Then sit back, shut up and listen. Allow the candidate to speak, do not interrupt their flow. Encourage the person to speak by remaining silent, nodding or making appropriate continuation noises. Make a mental note of any areas on which you require more detailed information. When the interviewee has finished, ask questions to clarify any particular points.

Do not ask hypothetical questions which are beyond the experience of the person: as the American folk singer Joan Baez once said, 'Hypothetical questions get hypothetical answers'. There is a saying that 'past behaviour is the best indication of future behaviour'. Thus it is quite acceptable to ask such questions as, 'The last time that a customer complained to you about the products or delivery, how did you deal with this?'

Avoid old tricks such as handing the candidate a pen and asking him or her to sell it to you. It is a meaningless exercise. Similarly, do not be tempted to ask leading questions such as 'You would agree, wouldn't you, that...?' You will only get the answer you expect.

Remember, the object of this part of the interview is to let you assess the candidate's ability to do the job and fit in with the team. If the application form asks for information about hobbies and interests, ask one or two questions in this area. This will give you a clearer insight into the person's character.

3. Giving information
By the time you reach this point, you should have assessed the potential of the candidate. If you know that you will not be progressing this application, give the interviewee just a brief description of the job and the company. On the other hand, if you believe that the person is a good prospective employee, give him or her more detail. You must be the judge.

One sales manager said, 'Selling is a pressure business, so I always put candidates under pressure at interview, it tests their mettle!' First of all a selection interview is a completely different situation from a sales interview and secondly, selling is only a pressure business if the sales manager makes it so.

4. The next stage
Tell the candidate how and when you will be communicating your decision.

Checklist of good interviewing techniques
- Plan the interview carefully.
- Ensure that there are no interruptions, telephone calls and so on.
- Relax the candidate.
- Relax yourself, smile, look at the candidate.
- Begin with a 'Tell me...' question.
- Ask behavioural questions.
- Listen to the candidate's answers.
- Do not ask hypothetical questions.
- Ask permission if you wish to take notes.
- Do not harass or argue with the candidate.
- Do not be aggressive or put the candidate under pressure.

- Answer the candidate's questions clearly and concisely.
- Do not tell the candidate what a wonderful person you are.
- Give information about the job and the company as appropriate.
- Tell the candidate 'what happens next'.

Bad interviewing techniques
- No planning.
- Reading the application in front of the candidate.
- Interrupting the candidate.
- Being aggressive, putting the candidate under pressure.
- Answering the telephone, talking to other people.
- Not listening to the candidate.
- Writing copious notes.
- Talking too much.
- Getting side-tracked with matters unrelated to the object of the interview.
- Giving way to bias or prejudice.

MAKING YOUR FINAL SELECTION

Regardless of how scientifically you have conducted the interviews, subjectivity and gut feel will still affect your decisions. One of the main questions that you will have to answer is 'Can I work with this person?'

To help your selection, consider the following:

- Assess each applicant against the employee profile, not against each other.
- Only assess those points that you have checked.
- Make your assessment after each interview.
- Re-examine all your assessments after the final interview.
- Seek the views of other interviewers (if any).
- Select the candidate who most closely matches your employee profile.
- Do not select the best of a poor bunch, you will be inviting trouble later.
- If no candidate is suitable, re-examine your job description, employee profile and advertising copy.

QUESTIONS AND ANSWERS

Is the job description a legal document?

Provided that it was in existence at the time of a dispute, it can be used in evidence at an Industrial Tribunal.

I need to appoint a new Midlands rep, and would very much like to offer the job to a girl in our sales office. She is very keen to be appointed, but I am concerned that some of our customers may not take to a female representative, and also that she may accuse me of sex discrimination if I do not appoint her. What should I do?

Your first duty is towards your company. Advertise the job in the normal way, inviting her to apply. Undertake the recruitment process and if she proves to be the best candidate, offer her the job. However, if you select a more experienced male applicant, she will have difficulty in proving sex discrimination on your part.

My Sales Director has recommended the son of a friend as an applicant for a vacancy in my sales team. How should I deal with this?

Treat the son as you would any other candidate. Don't allow yourself to be pressured into giving him the job if he is not the best candidate.

EXERCISES

1. Prepare advertising copy for your own job.

2. You are faced with a candidate who possesses all the qualities that you are seeking. However, he is ten years older than you, has more industry experience and was a regional sales manager with a competitor until made redundant six months ago. Do you offer him the job?

6

Managing Training & Development

THE ROLE OF TRAINING

One of your most important functions as sales manager should be to train and develop your salespeople. It is often said that one of the first things you should do upon appointment is to develop your successor.

Many large companies have their own training departments who will provide formal sales training for your staff. If that is the case, you should not wash your hands of training, for that will only be the beginning. You will be expected to continue the practical training throughout each person's career with you. It is also essential that you have a thorough knowledge of and agree with the training being provided.

Practically everything a sales manager does should contribute towards the development of the sales team.

UNDERSTANDING THE IMPORTANCE OF INITIAL TRAINING

Induction training

Induction means 'leading into...'. Induction training is possibly the most important training as it will set the scene for the new employee. Regrettably, this is too often overlooked and is either scant or completely absent.

Induction training should be properly planned and start from day one. So what should it include?

ELEMENTS OF INDUCTION TRAINING

- Welcome by you – this task must never be delegated.

- Introduction to the team – of course this will not be possible if they are out of the office.

- Introduction to other people in the company with whom the new salesperson will be in contact with – this should include the managing director and sales director.

- Tour of company facilities, factory, warehouse, restaurant, toilets and so on.

- Discuss and agree the job description, territory, targets and administration.

- Company policies and procedures.

- Product/service training.

- Sales support – advertising, promotion, sales literature.

- Assign the new sales person to a 'mentor' – this person should be an experienced member of your team who has been thoroughly briefed.

- Initial sales training where applicable (see below).

Whatever you do, avoid:
- Being absent when the new person arrives.
- Leaving the person sitting at a desk with nothing to do.
- Telling the individual to find their own way round.

It can be very demotivating to the new employee if he or she believes that they are not being extended the courtesy and attention that they deserve. It is not unknown for people who experience this 'welcome' to leave the company at the end of the first day. If they do, it's your fault.

The role of the mentor
The dictionary definition of mentor is 'wise and trusted adviser and helper (of inexperienced person)'.

Invite your most appropriate sales rep to act as mentor to the new employee, brief him or her thoroughly and ensure that they are available to meet the person on the day that they arrive.

The mentor should:

- Help with the product/service training.
- Offer help and guidance where required.

- Assist with administration.
- Take the new person on customer visits.
- Accompany them on their initial sales visits.
- Monitor the person's progress and discuss it with you.

The ideal person to act as the mentor should be your Assistant or Deputy Sales Manager, if you have one.

ORGANISING FORMAL TRAINING

Formal sales training methods
Formal sales training normally takes place in a specific training environment and usually lasts between one and five days. The needs for such training will of course depend upon the requirements of the delegates. These can be both basic sales training for new and inexperienced sales people or refreshers for the more experienced. The three methods of providing this type of training are:

1. In-company training course.
2. External training course.
3. Self-generated.

In-company training
Advantages
- Each sales person will receive the same training.
- Conducted by experienced trainers.
- The participant will meet people from other sales teams in the company.
- It should be a motivating experience.
- Saves you time.

Disadvantages
- A place on a course may not be available when required.
- The method and content of the training is out of your hands.
- Some people do not perform well on formal courses.

External training
Advantages
- Plenty of choice available.
- Should be able to attend a course when required.
- Opportunity to mix with people from other companies.

Disadvantages
- Unless you have attended the course, you will not be aware of the method and content of the course.
- The course may not be pertinent to your products/services.
- Cost – more expensive than other types of training.

Self-generated training
Advantages
- You decide the course content and methods of training yourself.
- You have close contact with delegates and are able to monitor their progress.
- Training can be timed to suit individual requirements.

Disadvantages
- Very time consuming.
- Insufficient delegates to make it viable.
- Lack of formal training experience.

Although training is a vital function of sales management, it is advisable to gain experience through conducting short training sessions as part of your sales meetings, before embarking upon a full course.

TRAINING IN THE FIELD

How to carry out effective 'field' training
Every sales manager should spend a large part of his or her time accompanying their sales people on sales visits. These visits should be field training time. There is a tendency for many sales managers to concentrate their visits on the new and less experienced people, allowing the experienced ones to get on with it alone. While more of your time should be spent with the newer people, the others should not be forgotten because unknown to you they may be falling into bad selling habits.

Field visits should be motivating and well planned. They should be seen by the sales reps as an opportunity to develop their skills. Unfortunately too many people consider them to be a punishment. This is entirely due to the attitude of the manager.

Planning field visits
You should plan your visits one month in advance and give your representatives as much notice as possible. Why not give each a copy

of your visit schedule? Although you should not interfere with your sales reps' own plans, you can suggest to them any specific customers or prospects that you would wish to visit.

Although you will probably spend more time with the less experienced people, you should try to arrange at least one visit per month with each of your salespeople.

Before each day's accompaniment, discuss the programme and objective with each sales executive concerned. This will help both of you to have a more productive day.

What are the objectives of field visits?
- To ascertain the reps' strengths and weaknesses.
- To determine training needs.
- To monitor the results of previous training.
- To motivate the salesperson.

Golden rules of field visits
- Spend the whole day with one representative.
- Allow the person to decide where to meet you.
- Keep quiet during sales interviews unless invited to contribute.
- Never jump in to try to 'save' a sale. You will benefit more in the long term by helping the rep.
- Do not make notes during a sales interview.
- Discuss each interview as soon as possible after it has concluded.

At the sales interview
One of the major problems that sales managers experience is how to conduct themselves during a sales interview.

Introduction: Ideally you should be introduced as a colleague for once the customer realises your position, he or she will talk to you rather than the sales person.

Seating: If possible sit slightly behind your rep and out of the customer's direct eye-line.

Control: Ensure that control of the interview remains with the rep.

Questions: If asked a question, refer back to the salesman to provide the answer. Do not ask any questions.

Opinions: Do not be tempted to give your opinions even when asked to do so.

Example of a sales interview:
Cast: Jean Probert – Sales Representative
      Nigel Green – Sales Manager
      Bob Wilton – Customer

JP: Good morning, Mr Wilton. May I introduce my colleague Nigel Green from our marketing department?

BW: Good morning, please take a seat.

NG: Good morning, Mr Wilton.
(Nigel sits slightly behind and to the right of Jean.)

BW: So what is your role, Mr Green?

NG: I'm here simply to observe to see if there are ways of improving our service to our customers.

JP: I see from the trade press that you have recently won a contract to supply your products to Saudi Arabia. Congratulations! I trust therefore that you will need more of our switchgear equipment?

BW: Well, it's possible, if we can agree a good price.

JP: I'm sure we can. What sort of price are you seeking?

BW: At the moment, I think we pay £230 each, so we would want a discount.

JP: How many additional pieces will you be buying over the next six months?

BW: I don't know exactly, but it would probably be about a hundred and fifty.

JP: If you can guarantee that figure, we could offer an additional 7½ per cent.

BW: I was looking for something nearer 12½ per cent.

JP: I see, that's something we will have to look into.

BW: Also, because of lack of storage space, we would want delivery on a just-in-time basis. Is that possible, Mr Green?

NG: I'm sure Jean can answer that for you.

JP: If you provide us with an accurate schedule of your requirements, then we can arrange deliveries to suit.

BW: Yes we can do that. We just need to agree the price and the business is yours.

JP: Good. As we will have to hold stocks on your behalf and there will be higher delivery costs, I think 7½ per cent is a fair discount.

BW: How about if the 7½ per cent applies to all the items we buy from you, Mr Green?

NG: I must pass that back to Jean to answer.

JP: I appreciate your thinking, Mr Wilton. What we can do is to give you 8 per cent off the price for all additional products that you buy from us, over and above the existing quantity.

BW: I'll have to think about that. Put it in writing and I will phone you within the next couple of days.

JP: Alright Mr Wilton, I'll do that for you. Thank you for your time. Goodbye. (Jean and Nigel shake hands with Mr Wilton and leave.)

Note
In the above example, Nigel Green maintained a remote role. When asked a question by the customer, he passed it back to Jean Probert without becoming directly involved or offending Mr Wilton. This allowed Jean to retain control of the interview. If Nigel had answered the questions, Jean's credibility with the customer would have been reduced and Mr Wilton would probably have insisted on dealing directly with Nigel in the future.

Post interview assessment
This should happen as soon as possible after the interview. Traditionally, it takes place in the car. However, the proximity between the two people can be too close for a relaxed assessment. It may be better to hold the discussion over a cup of coffee.

As previously mentioned, you should not take written notes at the interview, however, it is useful to have a checklist to use during the assessment. The checklist will provide you with an 'aide memoire' and as a means of rating each part of the interview. An example of a typical checklist is shown in Figure 9. A good assessment should contain the following:

- Ask the rep's opinion of the interview.
- If the rep's opinion differs from yours, ask questions.
- Praise the good points.
- Ask the rep what they could do to improve the poorer points.
- Offer suggestions for improvements only when necessary.
- Agree your ratings with the rep.
- Agree an action plan for future visits and/or training.

FIELD VISIT CHECKLIST

Name *JEAN PROBERT* ....

Date *12 JULY 200X* ....

Rating:
1 – Poor
2 – Below Average
3 – Above Average
4 – Good

Comments

	1	2	3	4	
Introduction of manager		✓			
Opening the interview			✓		
Establishing rapport				✓	
Asking questions			✓		
Answering questions			✓		
Giving information			✓		
Presenting benefits			✓		
Using visual aids					N/A
Dealing with objections		✓			
Negotiating skills		✓			
Closing the sale		✓			

Action Plans:

Fig. 9. A field visit checklist.

DO NOT use the assessment as an opportunity to criticise your sales rep. Nobody will respond positively to criticism unless it is very constructive. If you do criticise, then don't be surprised if the rep switches off. The rest of the day will be a complete waste of time.

Example of post-interview assessment

The assessment of the above interview might go something like this:
Scene: Jean and Nigel are sitting at a table in a café drinking coffee.

NG: How did you think that interview went?

JP: Not bad. I don't think I could have done much more in the circumstances.

NG: Good. Let's look at it bit by bit. What about the opening?

JP: I suppose I could have given a clearer reason for you being there so that Mr Wilton didn't have to ask you. Otherwise I thought it was OK.

NG: Yes, I agree with you, we'll have to practise a smoother introduction. I particularly liked your early reference to his newly won contract. That got his attention right from the start and gave you a good reason for being there. That was excellent, well done. Now, what happened next?

JP: He asked about the price and I asked him how many extra units he would be buying.

NG: Yes, that was absolutely right and he gave you an answer and you offered him a discount and then what happened?

JP: He asked for a better discount which I didn't think we would give him, so I left it there as I didn't want to start 'horse trading'.

NG: You did absolutely the right thing there. Any other points?

JP: He started talking about scheduled deliveries.

NG: Yes and you agreed to his requirements. On reflection is there another way you could have handled that?

JO: No, I don't think so. Why?

NG: Can our production people meet the requirements?

JP: Ah, that's a good point. I'll check as soon as I get back.

MONTHLY FIELD VISIT ANALYSIS

Month.............................

	Sue Beaumont	Jim Evans	Andy Grimshaw	Paul Morton	Jean Probert	Chris Saunders
Introduction of manager	3	4	3	2	2	3
Opening the interview	3	3	2	3	3	2
Establishing rapport	2	3	4	3	4	3
Asking questions	3	3	3	3	3	2
Answering questions	2	3	3	3	3	2
Giving information	3	4	3	3	3	3
Presenting benefits	2	4	4	3	3	3
Using visual aids	3	4	3	4	N/A	2
Dealing with objections	2	4	3	3	2	3
Negotiating skills	2	3	2	2	2	1
Closing the sale	2	2	3	2	2	1

Fig. 10. A monthly field visit analysis.
It indicates that there is room for improvement in both closing and
negotiating skills. The manager can thus include training on one of
these topics during the next sales meeting.

NG: Fine. Then you returned to the matter of discounts.

JP: I pointed out the extra costs to us of making more frequent deliveries to try to get him to appreciate that 7 ½ per cent was a good offer.

NG: Yes, that was quite right, but then he asked for that to apply to all of his purchases from us.

JP: I could see this being a sticking point so that's why I offered 8 per cent.

NG: What did you ask for in return?

JP: Nothing.

NG: What could you have asked for? Remember, the art of negotiation is to always get something for something. Trade concessions.

JP: That's true but I don't know what I could have got from him.

NG: What are his present credit terms?

JP: Thirty days. Oh yes, I could have asked for payment within say twenty one days instead.

NG: Good. That's something to remember for the future, isn't it? Do you think we will get the business?

JP: Oh yes, Mr Wilton is a pussy cat really.

NG: Good, but just remember all pussy cats have claws. Overall I believe that you handled the situation very well. Where are we going next?

Comment
Whenever possible you should encourage your sales executives to identify and suggest improvements to their performance. If no suggestions are forthcoming, then offer a prompt, as in the case of credit terms in the above example. At the end of every month, you should analyse the field visit checklists. From this you will be able to discover any common training needs which can then be dealt with at a formal training session as part of a sales meeting.

Monthly Team Training Analysis
To help you in this, why not produce a Monthly Team Training Analysis, similar to that shown in the example (Figure 10).

TRAINING AT SALES MEETINGS

One sales manager always includes a short, formal training session at her monthly sales meetings. She identifies the topic from analysing the checklists of the previous month's field visits and from general observation of her sales team's activities. She often invites one of her team to prepare and conduct the training. Those asked are usually people who require training in that particular subject and she will of course help them to prepare the session. She finds that this approach has many advantages:

- It promotes teamwork and participation.
- It helps to develop people to train others.
- Those invited to perform will invariably work hard to ensure that they put on a good show for their colleagues.
- It helps people to help themselves.
- It relieves the manager of the burden of training.

Planning the session
- Seek an appropriate topic.
- The session should be between 30 and 45 minutes, depending upon the amount of group participation.
- Prepare your own 'prompt' notes.
- Prepare visual aids such as OHP slides, flip charts and videos.
- Prepare exercises for group activity.
- When you have prepared all the material, rehearse the session.

Here is an example of a typical training session designed for inclusion in a sales meeting.

Topic: Dealing with objections
1. Each delegate is given a sheet of paper containing ten typical objections. They are asked to identify each by type and to write down how they would handle it (5 mins).

2. The trainer leads a discussion, taking each objection in turn and writing the correct answer on a flip chart (15 mins).

3. Delegates are invited to put forward other objections that they have difficulty in dealing with. The group will discuss each one and offer solutions (10 mins).

4. Trainer will summarise the session (3 mins).

This approach allows everyone to participate and use their experiences to help their colleagues. At the same time it puts the least strain upon the trainer and so is suitable to be run by a member of the sales team. Your sales people, particularly the more experienced ones, are more likely to respond positively to short, formal training sessions devoted to one topic, than they are to a full day of training.

TRAINING FREELANCE SALESPEOPLE

Many companies have commission only sales representatives and sales agents to promote their business. These people are normally self-employed and therefore more independent than sales executives actually employed by the company. Nevertheless they should not be ignored when it comes to training.

Upon appointment, all freelance salespeople should attend an induction training programme which may also include product training. Usually they will expect a financial incentive and/or expenses for attending courses. You should undertake field visits and training in the same way as you would with employed staff. To overcome any reluctance on the part of freelance salespeople to attend training courses, it may be necessary to stipulate a required number of training days within the contract. It is easier to exercise control over the self-employed sales representatives if they are paid a small retainer.

If any of your commission only sales executives refuse to attend training courses for whatever reason, the likelihood is that they are not fully committed to your company and it may be wise to dispense with their services.

QUESTIONS & ANSWERS

How can I deal with the sales representative who constantly resists field accompaniment?

Arrange an informal interview with this person to review his/her progress. Use it to ask questions to discover the reasons for this resistance.

What should I do when I can see the opportunity for a sale slipping away during a field visit?

You must resist the temptation to jump in and 'save the situation'. If you do, your salesperson will lose all future credibility with that customer.

How can I develop the mature, experienced sales executive?

Discover, through conversation, what motivates that person. As a result, you may be able to delegate one or more of your tasks such as formal training sessions, mentoring or analysing marketing information.

What can I do about the salesperson who fails to respond to training?

First, take a close look at your training methods. Are they right for this person? Discuss with the person their thoughts and feelings about selling as a career for them.

How can I apply training and development to commission only sales people?

Obviously this is more difficult as you are not able to exercise as much control over them. Training should be offered and the benefits explained. However, it is up to the individual to accept it or not. If a salesperson does not attend training and fails to perform to standard, then you have grounds for dismissal if necessary.

EXERCISES

1. Prepare a field analysis sheet suitable for your own sales team.

2. Prepare an induction programme for your new salespeople.

3. You have recently been appointed as manager of sales staff who have never received field accompaniment from your predecessor and do not believe that they need it. How will you introduce a programme of field visits?

7

Motivating Your Team

UNDERSTANDING MOTIVATION

Motivation is a subject about which much has been written and discussed over the past decades. Many theories have been expounded by the likes of Maslow, Hertzberg and MacGregor and one would not dispute their content. Being psychologists, their theories were based on this branch of science. However, companies are bound by certain rules, regulations and expectations, so these theories often fail to work as intended, because managers were unable to satisfy the needs identified.

At one time it was thought that all motivation could be injected from outside; however, motivation is about personal needs which come from inside the individual. People have needs which require to be satisfied and they will only be motivated if the end result is satisfaction of one or more of these needs. Therefore managers can only motivate individuals effectively if they know that person's needs. These can often be observed by the person's behaviour.

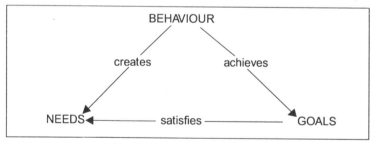

Fig. 11. Cycle of motivation.

Example

If a person needs additional money in order to behave in such a way as to obtain that mon overtime or taking an evening job. When they goal (the required money) they will be able to paying off the debt.

Needs, which are essential, should not be confused with wants, which are desirable. If you attempt to motivate someone by satisfying a want, that person will weigh up the extra effort required before deciding whether to accept the challenge or not.

IDENTIFYING NEEDS

As mentioned above, observation will provide a good indication of whether a person is motivated or not. Many people are self-motivated, which means that they make the effort to satisfy their needs and maintain the required level of satisfaction, and give outward signs of this fact. Those who are less motivated also give out signals to this effect.

Positive signs
- smart appearance
- cheerful expression
- maintain good eye contact
- carry out tasks willingly
- cooperative
- volunteer suggestions and ideas
- react positively to requests and new activities
- accept constructive criticism well
- neat and tidy.

Negative signs
- defensive body language
- uncommunicative
- monotonous tone of voice
- responds to criticisms and requests with 'Yes but...'
- poor time keeping.

As a manager, it is essential to talk to each member of your team to ascertain their particular needs, even those who appear to be well motivated. It is only then that you can apply the right motivations.

Although you should never assume what motivates anyone, you can make some calculated guesses depending upon the age and experience of the individual. For example:

of young salespeople
basic rate of pay

- time for personal activities
- good prospect of promotion
- high level of interest and job satisfaction
- help and guidance when requested.

Needs of experienced salespeople
- status within the team
- additional responsibility
- ability to work without interference
- recognition for effort and results
- respect from manager and colleagues.

SATISFYING NEEDS

It is a popular myth that everyone, especially salespeople, is motivated by money. We all have basic needs and expect that we will receive a salary that is sufficient to meet these needs. So salaries are not motivators in themselves. Commission only salespeople will be motivated by money up to the point where they have earned enough to satisfy these basic requirements.

Everyone has different needs, that is why one can motivate only individuals and not groups or teams. While you may not have the authority to satisfy specific needs such as more money or promotion, there are four areas of need of which everybody will have at least one:

- **Reward** – People like to be rewarded for achievement and effort. This need not be in the form of money or gifts. Sincere and genuine praise can often be sufficient. To be effective, praise should be specific. 'Thanks very much for getting that report to me on time, Bill: it was very helpful.' Follow this up with a handwritten note to reinforce the reward. Remember to give praise for effort as well as result.

- **Responsibility** – Many people need to feel responsible for a task or job, for which they have complete control and authority. You can satisfy this need by good delegation. Ask one of your team to provide specific market information or design a better control system.

- **Respect** – Everyone needs to be respected for what they are and for what they can contribute. Encourage and listen to people's ideas and suggestions. Involve your sales team in making decisions, especially those that will affect them. An example of this is to get them involved in setting targets. Take an interest in them as individuals, find out about their outside interests.

- **Recognition** – Probably the most important motivational factor. Everything that one does is aimed at satisfying this need, to be recognised by others. Whether it is securing a new account, getting paperwork in on time or being the top salesperson in the team, each is to satisfy the need for recognition. So make sure that everyone is made aware of each person's achievements.

OFFERING INCENTIVES

Although most salespeople have a competitive streak in their nature, it does not mean that they will always respond positively to competitions. Sales executives will only take part in competitions if:

- they need the prize on offer
- the extra effort required does not outweigh the value of the reward
- they need the recognition of being seen to be the best, irrespective of the prize.

One of the major problems with competitions is that they are too long in duration and those people who are lagging behind at the half-way stage will become demotivated, knowing that they cannot possibly win.

Case study
A publishing company decided to hold a competition for its sales representatives. The prize was a long weekend in a European capital of the winner's choice. However, the competition was based on the promotion of specific titles from the publisher's list. Those salespeople who were already doing well with those particular books were delighted, while those who were not so successful with those titles were immediately demotivated. As a result only a few of the team actually competed whilst the remainder just plodded along. The eventual winner only won by a small margin and although she was very pleased with her prize, those sales representatives who just failed were far from happy.

If you plan to run an incentive scheme then ensure that there are a number of different types of reward on offer and that everybody gets something (see Table 5).

Reward	Examples
Financial	Cash, bonus
Recognition	Trophies, special ties and scarves
Gifts	Merchandise, vouchers
Special events	Holidays, weekends away, theatre trips, dinner, gliding, ballooning, go-karting

Table 5

Team incentives

Instead of offering individual incentives which may promote ill feeling within the sales team, why not consider team incentives? A reward for the whole team upon achieving specific results. This should encourage cooperation within the team with everyone contributing to the overall results.

Ideal rewards in which the whole team can take part include go-karting, day trip to Paris or Brussels on Eurostar, theatre trip and horse racing. If you can afford to include the team members' partners in these events, so much the better.

CREATING THE RIGHT ENVIRONMENT

The working environment and relationship with their manager have considerable impact on an individual's motivation. There may be a number of things that you can do to improve these areas. While such improvements may not in themselves make a person more motivated, it will certainly help to prevent demotivation.

Assessing yourself

Are you self motivated? Are you a good motivator of others? Are you committed to your objectives and your team?

By answering the questionnaire in Figure 12 honestly, you will be able to spot those areas where you may need to improve.

1 – Never; 2 – Occasionally; 3 – Frequently; 4 – Always

	1	2	3	4
1. I encourage people to use their initiative				
2. I discourage involvement in office politics				
3. I show my commitment to our objectives				
4. I give praise for effort as well as results				
5. I try to persuade rather than force people to act				
6. I ensure work is as enjoyable as possible				
7. I regularly talk with my team to discover their needs				
8. I give my team full information where possible				
9. I involve my team in making decisions as appropriate				
10. I show my trust and respect for the team				
11. I delegate tasks to the right people				
12. I encourage cooperation within the team				
13. I show loyalty to my team				
14. I deal with demotivation as soon as possible				
15. I revise systems to keep them relevant				
16. I react to failure by analysis and correction not blame				
17. I ensure that I meet each member of my team on a regular basis				
18. I listen carefully to complaints and problems from my team				
19. I make a conscious effort to improve my motivational skills				
20. I only hold sales meetings when necessary				

Scoring

20 – 40 You are probably demotivating rather than motivating your team. A lot of work is required on your behalf to improve your skills in this area.

41 – 60 You appear to practise much that is motivationally sound; however, a number of missed opportunities need working on.

61 – 80 If you have been honest with your answers, you are a good motivator. Keep it up!

Fig. 12. Assessing your motivational skills.

Assessing the systems

Administration is one of the major causes of demotivation amongst sales people. Is everything that you require of them really necessary? What could be done to make it simpler and easier? Does everyone know the reasons for the paperwork? Do you give your team regular feedback?

Encourage and listen to suggestions for improving the systems. If people have been involved in designing the systems they use, they are more committed to operating them.

Introduce lap-top computers, scanners and other technological aids where practical and make sure that everyone is fully trained in using them.

Assessing meetings

Team meetings should only be held when there is a good reason for them. Ensure that all meetings are well planned and stimulating (see Chapter 8).

Assessing training and development

A well trained team of salespeople will result in a more motivated team. Remember to train for the future not just the present.

Summary

To help you promote a motivational environment, consider the following points:

- maintain good two-way communications with your team
- encourage ideas and suggestions
- involve your team in making decisions, setting targets *etc*
- develop your people through good delegation
- provide training where necessary
- praise effort as well as result
- create a 'no blame' culture within the team
- encourage cooperation
- reduce stress where possible
- use the right management style
- treat your team with respect.

QUESTIONS AND ANSWERS

One of my sales executives wants promotion and has shown that she is ready for it. However, there are no opportunities at present in my company and I do not want to lose her to a competitor. What can I do?

Do you have an official assistant or deputy? Although this may not mean an increase in salary, the title and status may satisfy her immediate needs.

The senior management in my company appear to care little about the salespeople; this is affecting the morale of my team and some are threatening to resign. What can I do?

Arrange a meeting with the management and present the case for the salespeople. Emphasise the benefits of a well motivated team and highlight the dangers of a demotivated one. Suggest ways in which the management can demonstrate that the salespeople are vitally important to the success of the company.

One of my sales representatives has recently shown signs of demotivation but is reluctant to discuss the matter. What can I do to resolve the issue?

When did these signals first emerge? Ask the person if anything happened or changed at that time. They may open up to you. If not then try to create as motivating an environment for them as possible.

EXERCISES

1. What would be the best ways of motivating each member of your sales team?

2. What 'incentive scheme' could work for your team without leaving anyone feeling demotivated?

3. One of your sales representatives is a lot older than you and has been with the company much longer. He has cultivated a small number of good customers with whom he spends most of his time. He resents any suggestions that he expands his customer base and is unwilling to take on additional responsibilities. He is a loner and does not appear to want to become part of the team. You are unhappy with his attitude, so what can you do to change it?

8

Managing Sales Meetings

INSIDE A RECENT SALES MEETING

I was recently invited to address a regional sales meeting for a company which manufactures electronic control equipment. The meeting was held at a hotel and was due to begin at 11.00am. I was allocated the first 30 minutes after lunch.

Those present were the sales director, the regional sales manager and nine sales representatives. At 11.00am precisely, the sales director opened the meeting, although two representatives had not arrived. He began by thanking everyone for attending and gave a brief outline of the meeting's contents. He then discussed a number of points including administration and the need to generate more new business. This was followed by a request for ideas for improving the sales side of the company. A lively discussion ensued with several people talking at once. We stopped for lunch at 12.30pm.

Promptly, at 1.30pm, I was introduced. I spoke on the subject of 'Buying Motives' for 25 minutes, allowing five minutes for questions. I was thanked by the sales director who then took his leave to return to head office for a further meeting.

It was now the turn of the regional sales manager, a large, bluff, enthusiastic man. He proceeded to present a series of new sales aids designed to help the sales reps, after which he introduced a new product for the sales force. This should have taken no more than three-quarters of an hour. However, each item was accompanied by numerous questions, mostly from the same small group of people, many of which only affected the questioner. Every question was treated to a lengthy answer, liberally sprinkled with personal anecdotes. The sales manager was the type of person who would never use ten words when a hundred would do.

At 4.00pm, he began to gather his papers together and hoped that everyone had found the meeting interesting. Naturally, we took this as a signal that the meeting was over. However, he then launched into a 30 minute ego trip, relating his experience of dealing with customers. I don't know if this was intended to motivate the sales reps, but looking round the room I noted, with few exceptions, that those present were becoming increasingly irritated with the *spiel* and were anxious to leave. That final half hour killed the meeting stone dead.

Analysis of the meeting

When I reached home, I analysed the meeting as follows:

Good points
- Started on time.
- Comfortable meeting room with no interruptions.
- Adequate lunch, coffee and tea provided.
- Opportunity given to everyone to contribute suggestions.

Bad points
- No agenda issued prior to the meeting.
- Insufficient control from the chair during discussions.
- No control over questions.
- Answers too lengthy.
- No predetermined finishing time.
- The final 30 minutes.

WHY HOLD SALES MEETINGS?

A very good question. Far too many meetings take place purely as a result of tradition. 'We *always* have a meeting on Monday.' If this is the only reason, then the meeting should not take place. Such meetings tend to be unorganised, demotivating and a general waste of time. There must be a **defined purpose** for the meeting before it is arranged.

Sales meetings should only take place when there is a specific objective to achieve. They do not have to be held regularly if there is no reason. Very often a series of one-to-one meetings between the sales manager and each representative will serve the purpose, particularly if it is to discuss individual sales performances.

Reasons for sales meetings

A meeting of the whole sales team should only take place when the contents and objectives affect each person. For example:

- Introduction of a new product.
- Changes in company policy.
- Introduction of new systems.
- Request for ideas and suggestions –'brainstorming'.
- Training.
- Other changes which will affect everyone present.

PLANNING A SALES MEETING

There are several questions that you should ask yourself when planning a sales meeting.

- Why – why hold a meeting? What are the specific reasons for it?
- What – what do I want to achieve? The objectives?
- Who – who should attend? Who will benefit from attending?
- When – when is the most convenient time for all to attend?
- Where – where should it be held? — the most suitable venue.
- How – how should the topics be best presented for maximum effect?

Why
You should have clear reasons for calling the meeting. These should fall into one or more of the above categories.

What
Define the objectives carefully. What do you want the attendees to take away from the meeting: knowledge, skills, sense of involvement?

Who
In addition to the sales team, are there any other people within the company who could benefit from attending? Who is best suited to present each topic?

When
Which day of the week will cause fewest disruptions? Friday afternoons are not universally popular and can be demotivating.

Where
If possible hold the meeting away from the office. This will reduce the likelihood of interruptions and generally will be more motivating for the sales team, especially if they are scattered throughout the country.

AGENDA

Purpose: Introduction of new product

Date: 14th January 200X

Start time: 9.30am.

Finish time: 12.15pm.

Venue: Conference Room 1.

Participants: The sales team

                Jim Walker – Product Development Manager

                Lynn Veasey – Marketing Manager

                Paul Roberts – Sales Manager

Topics: 1. Presentation of new product – Jim Walker
                   (45 mins)

                2. Advertising and promotion – Lynn Veasey
                   (30 mins)

                3. Selling strategy – Paul Roberts (45 mins)

                4. Training: Presenting the new product to
                   prospects (15 mins)
                   Dealing with possible objections (15 mins)

                5. A.O.B. (10 mins)

Please advise Paul if you have any points that you wish to raise under
A.O.B.

Fig. 13. An agenda for a sales meeting, showing the correct headings.

How
How should each topic be presented: verbal presentation, workshop, syndicate exercises, video?

Setting agendas
Every sales meeting should be preceded by an agenda. This is a synopsis of the meeting which the organiser of the meeting should prepare and distribute to all concerned at least 48 hours before the meeting. Always give your salespeople as much notice as possible of an impending meeting. This will enable them to plan their activities accordingly.

Each agenda should contain the following information:

- title and objective
- date
- venue
- start time
- participants
- topics with timings and presenter
- finish time.

An example of a typical agenda for a sales meeting is shown in Figure 13.

Any other business
This is the bane of every meeting as it so often degenerates into a general free-for-all and is a great time waster. To prevent this happening, it needs to be very carefully controlled. To help you manage it, here are some suggestions:

- Ask the participants to advise you of any points they wish to raise, well before the meeting takes place.

- Decide which items to include. They should only be those that are pertinent to the majority of participants. Personal matters should be dealt with outside the meeting.

- Allow a specific amount of time for AOB and keep within it.

- There is a school of thought that believes this should be the first item on the agenda as it gets it out of the way before proceeding with the main purpose of the meeting.

- Maintain strict control over supplementary questions.

CONDUCTING A SALES MEETING

Every meeting should have a chairperson. This will normally be you, the sales manager. However, depending upon the purpose of the meeting, it can be advantageous to appoint one of your sales representatives to the chair. You may be pleasantly surprised to discover how well that person exercises control over his or her colleagues.

The chairperson
The role of the chairperson is to:

- Open the meeting by defining the objectives.
- Introduce each topic and speaker.
- Control the timings.
- Ensure that questions are not hogged by one or two people.
- Decide whether or not questions should be dealt with at the meeting or afterwards.
- Make sure that the discussions do not drift from the point of the meeting.
- Summarise the meeting at frequent intervals.
- Agree all actions to be taken following the meeting.
- Close the meeting on time, with a summary of what has taken place.

A chairperson should not
- Dominate the discussions.
- Be critical or judgemental of points raised.
- Use the position to air his or her personal views.

Action plans
Most sales meetings will results in actions to be undertaken by those attending. In this case all such actions should be agreed between the parties concerned as follows:

- The reason and objective should be clearly defined.
- A standard should be agreed where applicable.
- A monitoring system should be set up if necessary.
- Authority should be given where needed, *ie* other people who

were not at the meeting, but who will be involved in the action, must be advised.
- When and how the results will be communicated to those concerned.
- The above should preferably be in writing to act as a record.

What makes a good sales meeting?

People should look forward to attending your sales meetings and regard them as of benefit, rather than a waste of time or an opportunity to have a good moan. Although you cannot ensure that everyone will have a positive attitude towards the meetings, you can help in these ways:

- Only hold meetings when they are really necessary.
- Prepare and distribute an agenda.
- Start and finish on time.
- Vary the methods of presentation.
- Arrange meetings at different venues in your region so that the same people do not have a long distance to travel. When using outside venues, remember to include the costs in your expenditure budget.
- Control questions and discussions.
- Make the meeting informative and motivating.
- Provide opportunities for involvement and participation.
- Don't make the meetings too long.

Sales conferences

Many companies hold annual or biannual sales conferences. These very often take place at a hotel and may last one or even two days. The objective is normally to review the past year's performance and encourage the sales force to do even better next year.

I have attended numerous such events over the years and they fall into two distinct categories, very good or diabolical. So what makes a bad sales conference?

The bad sales conference
- Poor venue – insufficient room, uncomfortable seating, poor lighting, lack of air conditioning, inadequate refreshments.
- Badly organised – no agenda, poor preparation, no control over timings.
- Too much criticism, not enough praise.
- Too many presenters, many of whom have no sales awareness.

- Too much talking at the audience.
- Little or no opportunity for participants' involvement.

Plan for success
Sales conferences require a great deal of planning and preparation. They should be expanded versions of the sales meeting. As well as ensuring that none of the above bad points occurs, the organiser needs to:

- thoroughly brief each speaker
- provide plenty of breaks for refreshment
- make sure that the conference ends on a high note.

Much will of course depend upon the budget allowed for the conference. If finances permit, it may be worth while seeking help from professional conference organisers. Similarly, it can be highly motivating to the delegates if the conference is hosted by a well known but suitable 'personality'. However, the main thing is to keep it entertaining and informative.

QUESTIONS AND ANSWERS

How do I control the person who constantly asks irrelevant or inane questions?

Avoid too much eye contact and encourage contributions from others. If you are obliged to deal with a question which is not relevant to the meeting, say that you will answer it after the meeting.

How do I deal with the know-all?

Invite the person to express their views to the meeting and their reasons for holding them.

Should minutes be taken at the meetings?

Generally, only for recording action plans.

I hate speaking to groups of people. How can I overcome this fear?

Prepare the meeting fully, make notes and rehearse your opening remarks.

EXERCISES

1. Prepare an agenda for your next sales meeting.

2. List the benefits and disadvantages of holding a sales meeting at a hotel.

3. Your sales director insists that you hold a sales meeting every Friday afternoon, even though many of your salespeople will have long distances to travel. How will you persuade him that it is not a good idea?

9

Managing Sales Forecasts and Budgets

As a sales manager, one of your main administrative tasks will be to formulate and control sales forecasts and sales budgets. The actual format may be determined by your company. However, you will still need to know how to construct and manage them.

WHAT IS A SALES FORECAST?

A sales forecast is simply a prediction of future sales over a given period of time. Sales forecasts can be expressed in terms of quantity of products or sales revenue. More often it is a combination of both.

There are three types of forecast:

- Short term – this normally covers the next 12 months.
- Medium term – usually between 1 and 3 years in the future.
- Long term – over 3 years.

The longer the term the less accurate the forecast is likely to be. However, it should indicate a general trend.

Why forecast?

The main purpose of a sales forecast is to enable the company to plan in various areas of its operation, such as:

- Production – how much needs to be produced? Will this require investment in new plant and equipment?

- Financial – what will be the company's inward cash flow? Will it need to borrow? Can it afford to invest? What will be the likely net profits?

- Promotion – what advertising campaigns will be necessary? How much can we spend?

- Workforce – will it be necessary to expand or contract the workforce?

In addition to providing these management benefits to the company, forecasts will also provide you with vital information to help you control the activities of your team and give both you and them standards to achieve.

HOW TO FORECAST

One sales manager used to say that, in his opinion, the best way to forecast was 'to cast the bones, usually those of unsuccessful salesmen'. There are, however, more effective and less violent methods which are common practice.

The 'line of best fit'
One traditional method is to base future sales figures on historical information. Plot the actual past figures on a graph, draw a line between them (known as the 'line of best fit') and extend or extrapolate the line to show the probable future sales.

Example
Let us assume that the sales revenue for the last six years has been as follows:

Year 1 – £200,000
Year 2 – £250,000
Year 3 – £225,000
Year 4 – £300,000
Year 5 – £275,000
Year 6 – £300,000.

The resulting graph would be as shown in Figure 14:

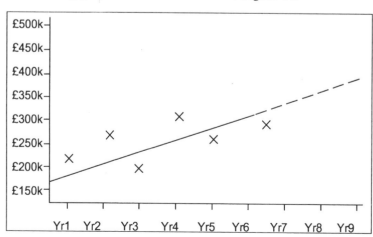

Fig. 14. Using a graph for sales forecasting.

From the above graph, we can now estimate the sales revenue for years 7, 8 and 9.

This method, which is most suited to medium and long term forecasting, is flawed because it assumes that everything else will remain equal. It never does!

In reality, we need to take many other factors into account.

- The overall economic situation – is the economy in recession, expansion or static?

- The market – is it expanding, declining or level? Has the market sector for your products changed? Are there new markets to be explored?

- The competition – are there more or fewer competitors? Why? What is the level of competitive activity? Have their prices changed? Are they spending more on advertising? Are more overseas competitors infiltrating your traditional markets?

- Your customers – what percentage of your business comes from what percentage of your customers? By what percentage have the number of your customers risen or fallen? How vulnerable are your major customers? How loyal are your customers?

- Your sales team – are they capable of gaining more business? Will they require more training? How committed are they?

- Trends and fashion – have your company's products been superseded by better and more efficient products? Are your products seasonal or subject to whims or fashions?

- Production department – are they capable of meeting your forecast?

How do you obtain this information? Much of the general data can be gained from reading the trade press and newspapers. For detail about more local markets, customers and competitors, you must rely on and encourage your sales team to provide it for you.

How do you use the information? Begin with the historical figures to give you a sales trend. Then adjust this according to the information you have available. Suppose your graph indicates an annual increase of 15 per cent, but your information tells you that the market is shrinking by 5 per cent per annum and one of your major customers is about to 'go to the wall'; in this case an increase of 7½ per cent is probably more realistic. When making sales forecasts, it is vital to be practical. There is no point in predicting high figures to impress your board – remember, you will be expected to achieve your targets.

If you have access to a computer with a sales forecasting model, then simply enter the past sales figures together with other information that you have received and the forecast will be produced for you. Be careful that the computer is not allowed to be more optimistic than you.

Short term forecasts

One of the best ways of producing a short term forecast is by involving your sales team. Ask each member to give you an estimate of their sales over the next six or twelve months, warning them to be practical and not over optimistic. The total of these figures will be the basis of your forecast. As the salespeople have been responsible for setting their own targets, they will be committed to achieving them.

Sales revenue cash flow forecast

Unless you are extremely fortunate, your customers will not pay for goods and services upon receipt. Most companies let their customers take a period of credit, say 30 days. However, when cash is tight, customers will extend this period for as long as possible. Therefore in order to obtain a more accurate prediction of when sales revenue will be received, you need to calculate the average length of credit taken.

This can be done with a simple formula:

$$\text{Days' credit} = \frac{\text{debtors}}{\text{annual sales revenue}} \times 365$$

For example a company with an annual sales revenue of £2,500,000 and debtors of £620,000 is giving

$$\frac{620,000}{2,500,000} \times 365 = 90 \text{ days' credit}$$

Thus you should forecast to receive sales revenue 90 days after the sale has been made and the goods or service delivered.

WHAT IS A BUDGET?

A budget is similar to a forecast in that it is an estimate of future income and expenditure. As a sales manager, your main concern will be with expenditure budgets, that is estimates of the cost of running your department over given periods of time.

Why budget?

It is essential to produce expenditure budgets in order to compare the cost of selling with the estimated sales revenue. This will show the amount of profit that you expect to make. (It may indicate that you will be operating at a loss!) Sales expenditure budgets are normally done on a monthly basis for a twelve month period. By comparing the actual expenditure with the budgeted expenditure, you will be able to keep control and make adjustments if necessary.

PLANNING THE BUDGET

Your budget headings

Firstly, you must decide upon the expenditure headings. These can include:

- salaries
- NI contributions and pensions
- commissions
- car expenses
- hotel accommodation
- telephone
- stationery
- promotion/advertising
- incidental expenses.

Salaries
These are set amounts and only change when salary increases are made, or number of staff increases or decreases.

NI contributions and pensions
National Insurance and pension contributions are normally calculated as a percentage of the salary. Your company payroll department will have the details.

Commission
A percentage of the sales revenue.

Car expenses
These can be divided into two types: running expenses (petrol, servicing and so on) and car cost. The latter will depend on how the company purchases cars, outright purchase, leasing, rental and so on. You may also have to allow for depreciation, an amount of around 20 per cent of the list price which is deducted each year. Your accounts department should be able to provide this information.

Hotel accommodation
Companies may either allow a fixed sum, say £50 per night, or reimburse the actual amount spent.

Telephone
Based on past costs with a percentage uplift.

Stationery
As for telephone.

Promotion/advertising
This should be based upon future promotional plans.

Incidental expenses
A sum to cover small, unspecified expenses not large enough to have their own headings.

Contingency
This is a sum to cover unexpected expenditure such as recruitment costs.

As with forecasting, past information should provide the basis for your future budgets. If for example the monthly car expenses were £300, by taking into account any price rises for fuel, servicing and so on you might decide upon a figure of £325 for this year's budget.

In some circumstances, you may be given one overall figure for the year's expenditure. Therefore you will need to allocate the amount to the various expenditure headings.

Rolling budgets
Your budget form should have three columns for each period:

budget, actual and variance. By comparing the actual with the budget, you will have a plus or minus variance. If the trend shows that the actual expenditure is greater than that budgeted, it would be sensible to adjust the budget for the future periods. This becomes a rolling or adjusted budget (see Figure 15).

If the actual expenditure is greater than the budget, you may need to investigate the reason for this. Is money being wasted? For example there could be too many telephone calls during peak times which could easily be made at other times. In such cases you will need to explain the situation to your salespeople, ask them to be more cost conscious and emphasise the possible results if they don't change their habits.

Budgeting for specific projects

During the course of the year, you may be expected to provide budgets for certain projects that are planned to take place. These can include exhibitions, promotional campaigns, additions to the sales team, setting up a tele-sales team and so on.

When faced with this, your first task is to list all the cost headings, remembering that other departments of the company may be involved. You will then have to estimate the cost for each item. This will mean obtaining as much information as you can from a variety of sources; some of the information may be historical if similar projects have been carried out in the recent past. Where applicable, you will be expected to forecast the additional sales revenue anticipated by the project.

As with the rolling budget, you will need three columns to compare actual costs with your budget. This information can prove vital when planning similar events in the future (see Figure 16).

Controlling costs

If it costs £20 to produce a product which is then sold for £30, one would expect the profit to be £10. However, we also need to consider the cost of making the sale: if this was £5, then the profit would only be £5.

Of these selling costs, some such as salaries and a contribution towards office expenses are **fixed costs** and must be recovered regardless of how many products are sold. Others, including travel, hotels and telephone are **variable costs** and depend upon the activity of the sales team.

Most sales managers have little or no control over the fixed costs, but they will need to keep control of the variable costs. For example, if the travel expenditure is higher than that budgeted, you will have

SAMPLE BUDGET

Item	January			February			March		
	Budget	Actual	Variance	Budget	Actual	Variance	Budget	Actual	Variance
Salaries	12000	12000	0	12000	12000	0	12000	12000	0
Commission	10000	10500	+500	10000	10750	-750	11000	11300	+300
Car Exp.	750	800	+100	1000	950	-50	1000	1400	+400
Hotel Exp.	900	900	0	1000	1200	+200	1200	1100	-100
Telephone	250	225	-25	250	200	-50	300	325	+25
Sundries	100	50	-50	150	120	-30	150	110	-30
Totals	24000	24475	+475	24400	25220	+820	25650	26235	+585
Sales Rev.	31000	32500	+1500	35000	34000	-1000	38000	40000	+2000

Fig. 15. A rolling or adjusted budget. We can see from the above that although actual expenditure exceeded budget by £1880, actual income exceeded forecast by £2500.

You have decided to hold a two day exhibition of your company's product range at a hotel in Edinburgh. It will be necessary to publicise the exhibition and send invitations to appropriate businesses in the area. Two 'agency' girls will look after your reception desk and you will provide tea, coffee and soft drinks for visitors. You produce the following budget:

BUDGET FOR EDINBURGH EXHIBITION

Item	Budget	Actual	Variance
Hire of venue	1500		
Accommodation	3750		
Agency fees	1800		
Refreshment	900		
Transportation	500		
Literature	450		
Postage	100		
Contingency	500		
Total cost	9500		

Fig. 16. A project budget.

to take a close look at the route planning of your salespeople. Maybe they are making unnecessary journeys or doubling back on themselves. In this case you should discuss with the people concerned, ways of improving their planning to reduce these costs. Similarly you should compare the costs of staying in hotels overnight with the cost of returning home instead. Are the minimum number of telephone calls made at peak times? Is it really necessary to treat certain customers to expensive lunches?

Often the sales team do not realise how their expenses are building up and you may only have to bring the matter to their attention to see an improvement.

QUESTIONS AND ANSWERS

Can I be held legally responsible if my sales team fail to achieve forecast or budget?

No. These are simply estimates to enable the company to plan.

What can I do if I am given a sales forecast by my board which I believe is unrealistic?

Prepare your own forecast based on the facts available to you and present this to your management. They may not change their figures but at least they will be aware of your position.

I suspect that one of my reps is fiddling his accommodation expenses. So far I am unable to prove it. I have warned the rep several times but the problem still exists. What can I do?

Before making any accusations, it is necessary to obtain proof. Make sure that receipts are obtained for all expenses claimed and only reimburse the receipted amounts. You may need to check with the hotels that the receipts are accurate and genuine. Alternatively, allow your sales reps a fixed amount to cover each night's accommodation, again requesting receipts as proof of expenditure. Make it clear to each rep what items they can claim for.

EXERCISES

1. You are a sales manager with a team of four salespeople. Your forecasts predict sales revenue for the next six months as follows: £25,000, £25,000, £30,000, £35,000, £20,000, £30,000. You receive a monthly salary of £1,500 and 5 per cent commission on all sales revenue. Each of your salespeople has a monthly salary of £1,000 plus 10 per cent commission on their sales. In addition each salesperson including yourself, has a car allowance of £500 and £200 per month to cover other expenses. You have estimated that it costs £15,000 per year to run the office.

    Prepare a budget for the next six months together with estimated profit.

    In reality, sales for each of the first two months are down by 5 per cent and you receive an unexpected order worth £5,000 in month five. Due to a motor accident, one of your salespeople is absent for the whole of month three. At the end of month three you are informed that office expenditure will rise by 10 per cent from the following month.

    Calculate the variances from your original budget and the actual profit earned together with any variance from that estimated.

2. Your company manufactures two products, called Hoppits and Toppits. It is now half-way through year 6. From the detailed information given below, produce a medium term sales revenue forecast to cover years 7, 8 and 9.

Units Sold

	Hoppits	Toppits
Year 1	100k @ £2 each	50k @ £5 each
Year 2	125k @ £2 each	70k @ £6 each
Year 3	175k @ £3 each	100k @ £6 each
Year 4	150k @ £3 each	80k @ £8 each
Year 5	160k @ £5 each	90k @ £9 each
Year 6 (to date)	75k @ £5 each	50k @ £9 each

One of your major customers, who purchases 10k Hoppits each year, has recently been taken over by a Japanese company and will no longer be buying from your company. The industry estimates that demand for Toppits will increase by 5 per cent per annum for the foreseeable future. Your prices will be increased next year: Hoppits will be £6 each and Toppits £10 each. Rumour has it that a large Italian manufacturer of Hoppits will be entering the UK market next year with a selling price of £4.50 each. Your company are working on an improved Hoppit which should be ready for sale at the beginning of year 8. You propose to expand your present sales team of five, by one additional salesperson at the beginning of next year. This will enable you to cover the country more effectively.

10

Managing Exhibitions

THE ROLE OF EXHIBITIONS

When a company decides to attend an exhibition as an exhibitor, it is very often the responsibility of the sales manager to organise and run the stand. If you find yourself in that position, this chapter should be of help.

Types of exhibition

There are three main types of trade exhibitions:

1. National and international.
2. Local, such as county shows and those organised by chambers of commerce.
3. Self-organised, where you are the sole exhibitor.

Why exhibit?

The main reasons for exhibiting are:

- To launch a new product or service.
- To meet customers and distributors.
- To enter new markets with existing products.
- For public relations.
- To maintain prestige.
- To undertake market research.
- Because the competition is there.
- To generate genuine enquiries.

Exhibitions can play an important part in a company's marketing plans because they are a meeting place on neutral territory for existing and potential customers. People attend voluntarily for a variety of reasons such as to:

- meet current and new suppliers
- enquire about new trade opportunities

- find new markets
- study new products
- compare existing products
- order new products
- gain technical knowledge
- get information about terms and prices
- obtain literature
- solve problems.

PLANNING THE EXHIBITION

Regardless of the type or size of the exhibition, a number of points must be taken into consideration when planning. Here is a useful checklist.

Your exhibition checklist
- Agree the budget – this will have a vital bearing on your subsequent planning.

- Reserve a site – try to select a position near an access point or other feature such as toilets or snack bar; this ensures that most visitors will see your stand.

- Design the stand. Unless you have experience of this, enlist the help of a stand designer. Use the space available intelligently, don't overcrowd it with products. If possible, set aside an area for discussing business with prospective customers.

- Appoint and brief a stand contractor to build the stand.

- Arrange for supplies of electricity, water and so on, to the stand.

- Agree which products are to be displayed.

- Arrange for transportation of equipment, products and so on to the exhibition site.

- Order stand furniture and other fittings.

- Plan staff requirements.

- Brief and train staff.

- Arrange hotel accommodation where necessary.

- Ensure supplies of product literature.

- Arrange for invitations to be printed.

- Prepare list of people to be invited.

- Send invitations.

- Plan advertising and publicity.

- Order tickets and badges.

- Place advertisement in exhibition catalogue.

- Prepare press releases.

As can be seen from the above list, there are many things to be done and each will require a date by which it should be completed. To help you with this, why not produce a schedule similar to that shown in Figure 17. This is often known as a **Gant Chart**.

Selecting staff
The number of people required to man your stand will depend on its size. The stand should appear neither overcrowded with salespeople nor under-manned.

You will probably involve all of your sales team (unless it is a small, localised exhibition, when you will only need the salespeople from the geographical area covered by the exhibition).

If your products are of a technical nature, it can be very useful to have someone from your research or production department present, to answer technical questions. You may also want a secretary to deal with the administration. You should appoint one person as the stand manager for each day. This need not be you; choose different members of your sales team for this responsibility. Apart from anything else it will help their own job development.

Training
You will need to train your salespeople in the following areas:

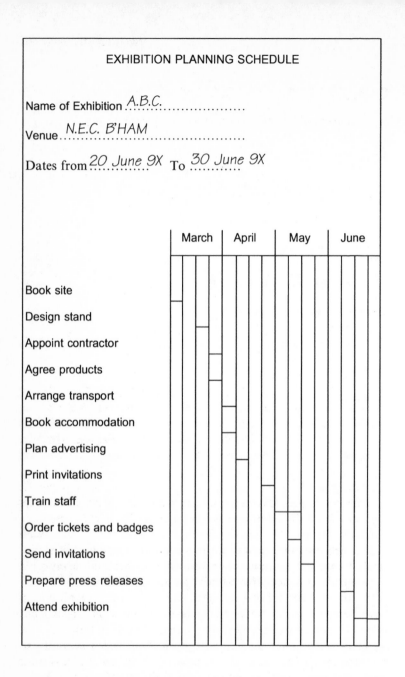

Fig. 17. An exhibition planning schedule.

- Location of the stand in relation to features such as access points, toilets, restaurants and so on. Give each person an exhibition plan similar to that shown in Figure 18.

- Familiarisation with the stand layout. A model, or at least a detailed plan, is essential for this.

- Knowledge of fire and safety regulations.

- Ensure everyone has full product knowledge.

- How to approach visitors to the stand. NEVER say 'Can I help you?' as this usually results in a negative response. The following suggestions are more likely to bring positive replies:
  – 'What are you particularly interested in?'
  – 'Who do you normally buy from?'
  – 'How does this compare with what you are using at present?'

- How to complete Enquiry Forms.

MANAGING THE EVENT

Staffing rota

As it is unlikely that every member of your sales team will be required to spend each day at the exhibition, prepare a rota showing who should attend and when. Ensure that everyone has as equal a time as possible on the stand. As exhibitions are very tiring for exhibitors, ask people to spend only half a day at a time on the stand if practical. Make adequate allowances for refreshment breaks.

Many years ago I was a salesman for a company that made accounting machines and office equipment. The company decided to exhibit at a large, international exhibition held at Olympia in London. The exhibition was to last ten days including the Saturday and all of the twelve salesmen were ordered to attend each day. The exhibition opened to the public at 10.00am and closed at 6.00pm. We were expected to be on site at 8.30am to ensure that the stand was tidy, and 'plan' for the day. Since the stand manager, who happened to be the sales director, held a post mortem at the close of each day, we rarely left before 7.00pm. We were allowed breaks totalling one hour each day, to be taken at the discretion of the stand manager. The stand was not particularly large and as we all stood there we resembled a group from 'rent-a-crowd'. Naturally, everyone was flagging by mid-afternoon and the atmosphere in the hall was

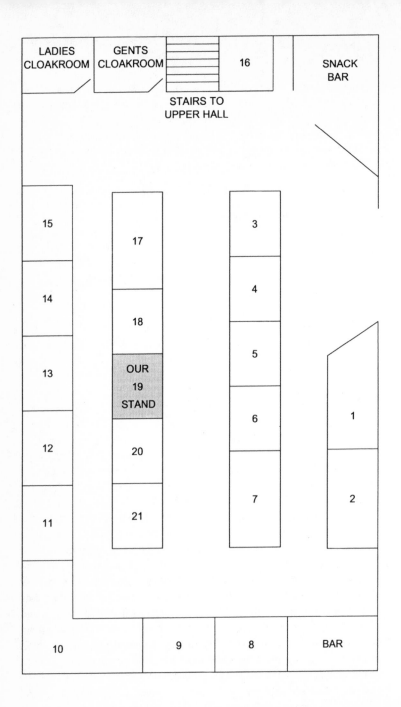

Fig. 18. A typical exhibition setting.

warm and dry. As the days wore on, the morale of the troop slumped to new lows and several salesmen developed mystery illnesses to avoid attending. On the eighth day, one salesman actually resigned from the company. Not unexpectedly, the exhibition was declared an unmitigated disaster for the company. The only good thing to emerge was that never again was the sales director put in charge of exhibitions.

Role of the stand manager

This person is responsible for the efficient running of the stand. The stand manager's duties are to:

- ensure full deployment of staff and that the rota is adhered to
- motivate the staff
- arrange refreshment breaks
- ensure that the stand remains clean and tidy
- make sure that there are sufficient supplies of sales literature and enquiry forms.

General stand tactics

Dos

- Show real enthusiasm for your stand, products and company.
- Wear your name badge at all times.
- Give visitors time to focus on a particular item.
- Acknowledge waiting visitors by a nod, smile or wave.
- Approach visitors 'head-on'.
- Try to discover the visitor's identity.
- Introduce visitors to other members of your staff by name.

Dont's

- Take a 'defensive' stance at the edge of the stand.
- Group together. Visitors do not like breaking up the party.
- Obscure exhibits or access to the stand.
- Occupy seats unless talking to a potential customer.
- Look bored or sit reading a newspaper.
- Set out sales literature in neat rows.
- Leave items on the floor; they can be dangerous.
- Pounce on visitors immediately they enter the stand.
- Hover near visitors.
- Neglect anyone.
- Leave dirty cups or glasses lying around.

ENQUIRY FORM
Name:
Position:
Company:
Tel. No:
Area of interest:

Fig. 19. A simple enquiry form for use at exhibitions.

Dealing with overseas visitors

As international trade increases and travel becomes easier, more and more overseas businessmen visit exhibitions, particularly the major ones. Whilst many of these visitors will speak English, many will not. Unless you have people able to converse in foreign languages, some difficulty may occur. To help overcome these, remember the following:

- Don't shout – their hearing is usually as good as ours!
- Speak slowly.
- Don't talk pigeon English; it sound ridiculous.
- Be more demonstrative than perhaps you would be with a UK visitor.
- Find out if translation facilities are available at the exhibition.
- If there is a group of visitors, speak to them through the member with the best English.
- Remember that your stand is the front line of your company's export market.
- If possible arrange to have your sales literature available in French, German and Spanish as well as English.

Enquiry forms

It is vital to make a record of the visitors to your stand, particularly those that showed an interest in your products. Hence the need for enquiry forms. These should be kept simple, yet provide all the necessary information (see Figure 19).

While on the stand, every salesperson should carry a supply and fill them in immediately after speaking to a prospect. They should then be placed in a box set aside for the purpose. At the end of each day, the stand manager should issue the forms to the respective salespeople, by area.

Companies sometimes give a small reward to the salesperson who records the highest number of enquiries each day. However, this usually results in many spurious enquiries. Quality is more important than quantity.

Following up enquiries

Don't wait until the end of the exhibition. Send details to prospective customers as quickly as possible, either from the exhibition or head office. Maintain the impetus of the enquiry to avoid the 'post exhibition anti-climax'.

Sales leads will need to be categorised into potential and urgent, so that priorities are established.

DEBRIEFING

At the end of the exhibition, you should arrange a meeting of all those concerned to evaluate the following points:

The exhibition itself
- Was it really relevant to your products?
- Were there sufficient genuine prospects?
- Were the organisation and facilities up to your requirements?

Your stand
- Was it in the right position?
- Was it the right size?
- Was the equipment exhibited in the right way?
- Were there enough seats?
- Was the stand sufficiently staffed at all times?
- Did you feel comfortable working on the stand?

The result
- Were enough enquiries generated?
- Was the quality of enquiries high enough?
- Is it worth repeating the exercise?

QUESTIONS AND ANSWERS

I want to organise a local exhibition of my company's products. How should I approach this?

Choose a suitable venue, preferably a hotel that has experience in running such events. It should be as central as possible within the area you wish to cover. Send personalised invitations to all those people you wish to attend. Otherwise follow all the above points.

How can I maintain contact between the exhibition and my office?

Many permanent exhibition halls have the facility for a telephone on the stand. If this is not available, you can use a mobile phone.

Do I need to be at the exhibition all the time?

No. However, it is a good idea to visit at least once a day to monitor progress and motivate your team.

EXERCISES

1. Prepare a schedule for a forthcoming exhibition, where you wish to exhibit your products.

2. What are the main differences between selling at an exhibition and selling directly to your prospects and customers?

3. How will you discourage 'time-wasters' and 'literature collectors'?

11

Managing Promotional Campaigns

Among your duties as sales manager, you may be expected to manage various types of sales promotional campaigns. As this is a specialised area of activity, this chapter should be of help to you.

HAVING CLEAR OBJECTIVES

Before embarking upon a promotional campaign, it is vital to be very clear about your objectives, as these can determine the type of promotion. Objectives include to:

- launch a new product/service
- make the public aware of your products/services
- persuade the public to buy your products/services
- heighten the profile of your company
- help your sales team to sell more.

Types of promotion

1. *Above the line*
   Media advertising, press, TV, radio and posters.

2. *Below the line*
   Anything that does not constitute media advertising:
   eg sales literature/brochures/catalogues
   direct mail
   exhibitions
   sponsorship
   public relations
   competitions
   'give aways'.

Let us now consider each of these in turn.

USING MEDIA ADVERTISING

Using an advertising agency

'What is the difference between an advertising agency and an Essex girl? One spends most of its time in pubs, is unimaginative and unreliable and leaves you feeling dissatisfied. The other is a girl from Essex.' Perhaps this is being a little unfair to advertising agencies, for they can be very useful. This will depend very much upon the agency that you choose and your budget.

When selecting an agency, try to find one that has experience with the type of products or services that you wish to promote and the market that you want to reach. You may feel more comfortable with a provincial agency rather than a large London company.

It is a fact of life that the larger your budget the more attention you will receive from the agency. If you approach a major agency with a budget of less than £50,000, you will probably be assigned a junior account executive. He or she may be very keen, but will probably lack the necessary experience. The best way to choose the right agency is to give a written brief of your requirements to three or four and invite them to present their proposals to you. Select the agency whose presentation most closely meets your needs.

What will an agency do for you?
- plan the campaign
- select the most appropriate media
- design the advertisement – including:
  artwork
  photography
  write the copy
- place the advertisements
- monitor the response.

Agencies are able to obtain favourable advertising rates from the media. However, these must be offset against their fees chargeable to you.

Planning your own advertising campaign

1. Decide which newspapers and journals you want to use.
2. Obtain information from the selected media:
   advertising rates
   readership/circulation
   type of readership.

3. Plan the campaign.
4. Design the advertisement.
5. Monitor the response.

Selecting the right media
There is a very wide range to choose from depending on the
objective of the campaign and the people you wish to reach:

● national, provincial and local newspapers
● magazines
● trade journals
● institute publications.

Newspapers and magazines fall into the category of **newstrade**. That
is, they contain a cover price and are purchased over the counter by
the public. Most trade journals are **controlled circulation** or **cc**. This
means that they are sent free of charge, on a regular basis to those
people that ask for them. This is known as **requested readership**. A
few trade journals such as *Farmers Weekly* and *Hotel & Caterer* are
not cc and are paid for by the reader.

The third category are those journals published by institutes and
organisations specifically for their members such as *The Director*
which is produced by the Institute of Directors.

Pros and cons
So what are the comparative advantages and disadvantages of each?

● As readers have to pay for the 'newstrade' media, they are likely
  to be read more thoroughly.

● It is more difficult to verify the quantity and type of readers of
  'newstrade' papers.

● Controlled circulation journals rely entirely upon advertisers for
  income.

● Normally, cc journals are only sent to readers with an interest in
  the subject matter.

● The quantity of cc journals actually distributed is audited on a
  regular basis by an independent bureau. This is known as the
  ABC figure.

- As cc journals are free to the recipient, it is difficult to tell how many people see each copy and how thoroughly they read it.

As advertising is expensive, it is a good idea to produce a comparison sheet of those journals which would be suitable for your advertisements. See Figure 20.

How to plan a campaign
Having decided *where* you wish to place your advertisements, you now need to plan *when*. This will depend upon:

- The objective of your campaign.
- Whether or not your products are seasonal.
- Major and local exhibitions.
- Competitive activity.
- Other promotional campaigns.

You will need to produce a media schedule (see Figure 21).

How to design your advertisement
Your budget will influence the overall design of the advertisement as you will need to consider the following:

- size
- colour
- photography
- artwork
- copy.

The most important lesson is to design the advertisement for the reader, not for yourself. Unless you have some experience at designing advertisements, you are strongly recommended to obtain outside help. See the book *How to Do Your Own Advertising*, in this series.

Printers and publishers have their own jargon surrounding advertisements, so here are a few terms to help you:
SPS – single page spread.
DPS – double page spread.
bleeding – the advertisement runs off the edge of the page without a margin.
gutter – the inside margin where two adjacent pages meet.
4 colour – full colour.

Title	Frequency	Format	Circulation	Type	½ page rate
The Farmer	weekly	A4	104,500	paid for	£1,050
Livestock	weekly	A4	32,650	paid for	£650
Arable Monthly	monthly	broadsheet	50,200	c.c.	£425
Pig World	monthly	A4	28,450	c.c.	£395
Farm Machinery	quarterly	A4	92,700	c.c.	£750
Market Gardener	monthly	A5	14,025	paid for	£250

Fig. 20. An advertising journal comparison sheet.
Note – to the best of the author's knowledge, all of the above titles and figures are fictitious.

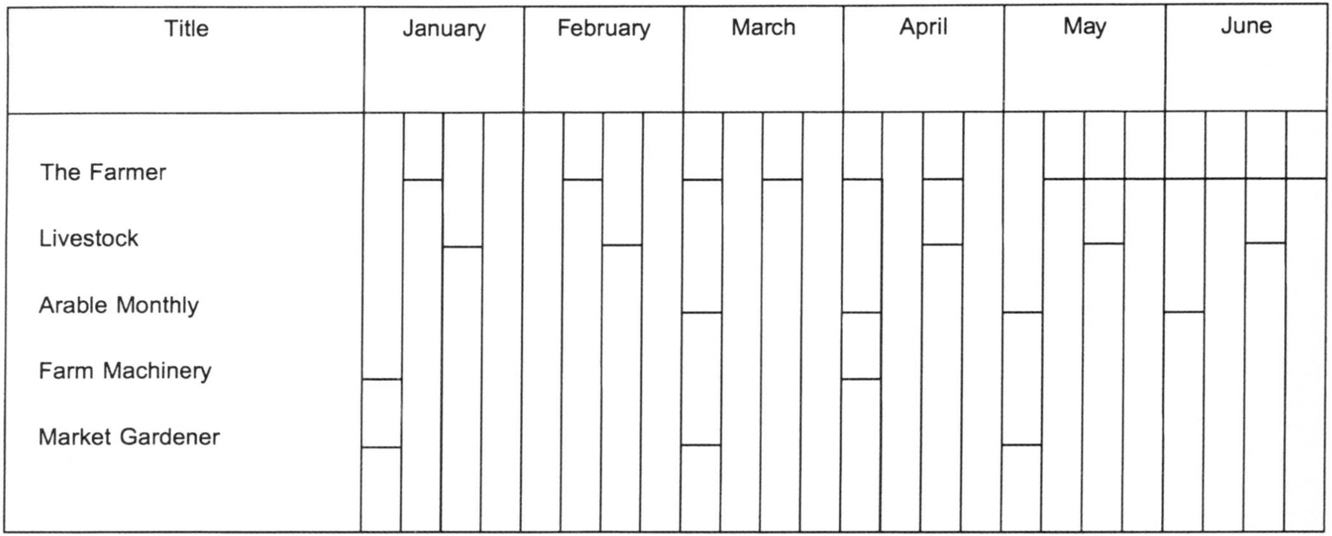

Fig. 21. A media schedule.

spot colour – a colour (such as red or blue) used in conjunction with black and white print.

ad/ed ratio – the number of pages devoted to advertising and editorial, *eg* '30/70'.

format – size of pages, *eg* A4, A5, broadsheet.

How to monitor response

It is extremely difficult to measure accurately the response to any specific advertisement. Although sales may increase following an advertising campaign, this may be partly due to other factors such as the economy, less competitive activity, changes in fashion and so on.

The only accurate measurements you can get are by inviting readers to order direct via a clip out **coupon** from the advertisement or by taking such a coupon to a retailer.

A number of trade journals offer a **Reader Enquiry Service**. This usually takes the form of a card which is included in the journal and lists the names of all of the advertisers in that issue. Readers are invited to tick those names from whom they wish to receive further information, and return the card to the publisher. In turn, the publisher passes this information on to the companies concerned. This will provide some measure of the effectiveness of the advertisement.

USING BELOW THE LINE PROMOTIONS

Using sales literature

Along with most other companies, you probably already have brochures of one sort or another. Ask yourself the following questions about the ones you currently use:

Who designed them?

When were they last updated?

Are they designed for the prospective customer?

Do they provide relevant information?

Do they contain too much or too little information?

Who uses them, how, when and why?

Do they meet the needs of your sales team?

What are the purposes of brochures?
Brochures are used in three different ways:

- sent in response to an enquiry
- sent as part of a direct mail campaign
- as a selling aid.

In most instances, the same brochure is used in each case. This means that either it is comprehensive enough to serve all purposes (and so is expensive to produce) or it is only suitable for one of the uses.

As you and your team will be the main users of sales literature, you should exercise considerable influence over its design and content.

Brochures that are used as part of a direct mail campaign need to be **teasers**. That is, they should contain sufficient information to tempt the recipients to contact your company for further details. Thus the content should:

- emphasise the benefits to the consumer of using your product or service
- keep technical data to a minimum
- be colourful and attractive
- be concise
- give the reader reasons to want more information.

Those brochures sent in response to enquiries should be similar to the above but should in addition:

- be aimed directly at the potential user of the product or service
- contain more technical information
- include testimonials from satisfied customers.

Tip
Always leave a few questions unanswered to encourage the reader to contact your company. Unfortunately, much of the sales literature requested ends up in the filing system in the buyer's office, so always telephone the company to discover who, by name, needs the information and send it directly to them. The brochures for your sales team should be comprehensive and do not necessarily have to be glossy productions. They are used to back up the information given at the sales interview.

Using direct mail

It is common knowledge that the average response rate to direct mail is typically only around 1½ per cent. A few companies such as *Readers Digest* and Damart, a clothing company, rely almost exclusively on direct mail for their business, and are very successful at it. However, they spend a great deal of time and money on designing their literature, and on postage. Whether or not you use direct mail to promote your business will depend largely upon the type of products or services that you offer. It undoubtedly works much better when directed at the personal consumer rather than at businesses.

As with advertising, there are a number of objectives for direct mail:

- to gain immediate sales orders
- to advise recipients of the availability of new and existing products
- to encourage sales enquiries
- to invite people to exhibitions and so on
- to keep your company name in front of customers and prospects.

As with any form of promotion, direct mail must attract the recipient's attention: it needs to be different from the normal 'run of the mill' junk mail that clutters so many letter boxes. If your budget allows, it would be wise to consult direct mail specialists for advice and help.

Using exhibitions

See Chapter 10 on how to organise an exhibition.

Using sponsorship

This is usually associated with large national and international companies who sponsor golf tournaments, cricket competitions, professional soccer teams and so on. However, smaller firms can gain much useful goodwill by sponsoring local events and teams.

Although you are unlikely to gain much business as a direct result of such sponsorship, it will certainly put your company's name in the public's mind. Localised sponsorship need not cost much. One of the cheapest ways is to sponsor a team of runners in a marathon or 'fun run'. All that is required is a set of T-shirts prominently displaying your company name or logo. A few hundred pounds will enable your company to associate its name with one or more events at a local cultural festival. Local sports teams will usually be delighted to display the name of the company in return for their sports kit.

If you decide to enter the world of sponsorship, simply approach the organisers of events that you wish to sponsor and negotiate a fee in return for your company name being associated with it.

Using public relations

The most common form of PR in business is to have an article about your company or products printed in the editorial section of a recognised journal or newspaper.

It is simply a matter of writing an article or press release and sending it to a journal for publication. Editors receive hundreds of such items and must exercise their judgement in which ones to print. Very few journals will reproduce articles in return for you buying advertising space as editors are very keen to retain their 'editorial integrity'.

You are best advised to employ the services of a PR agency. They will know the best journals and newspapers to use, the type of articles that attract editors' attention and the style of writing that is more acceptable. If, however, you would like to explore the possibilities of doing this yourself, see Peter Bartram's helpful book *Writing a Press Release* in this series.

Using competitions and 'give-aways'

This form of promotion is normally associated with consumer products, the object being to entice the customers to buy more of the product and encourage 'brand loyalty'.

The danger of introducing competitions with industrial products is that the market may consider them to be gimmicks and reduce the credibility of the company.

QUESTIONS AND ANSWERS

How can I persuade my company to let me run a local exhibition as they have never done so before?

You will need to prepare a full proposal showing the costs and the expected benefits and increased revenue. This must then be carefully presented to your sales director or whoever makes such decisions.

Our sales literature is designed and produced by the marketing department but is not suitable for our needs. How can I get it changed?

Arrange a meeting with the head of the marketing department. Explain why the existing literature is unsuitable and put forward your suggestions for improvement.

How can I predict the expected increase in sales from a direct mail campaign?

Unfortunately you can't, at least not with any accuracy!

EXERCISES

1. What, if any, improvements would you make to your existing sales literature, and why?

2. Select one of your products and write a 200 word article about it, suitable for publication in a trade journal.

3. List those publications in which you could place advertisements for your products or services. Obtain information such as advertising rates, circulation, type of readership and so on. Prepare a top five list in order of preference.

12

Managing Different Types of Sales Team

MANAGING COMMISSION ONLY SALESPEOPLE

An increasing number of companies are using commission only representatives to promote and sell their products. The obvious benefits to the companies are that they only pay on results, they do not need to provide a car or pay associated expenses and they are not concerned with National Insurance, pension schemes and so on. The disadvantage is that such salespeople are self-employed and thus independent and more difficult to manage and control.

To help you to manage commission only salespeople correctly, it is useful to know why they have chosen the commission based route rather than being employed: a question to ask at the recruitment stage. The responses may include:

- the prospect of unlimited earnings
- dislike of 'restrictions' of being employed
- able to take time off when they wish
- like being in control of their affairs such as taxation and pensions
- prefer to be independent.

This should give you an indication of what motivates the individual. Although some of these answers, such as taking time off, may not suit your requirements.

Controlling

This is the most difficult part of managing the self-employed salesperson. Some companies attempt to exercise control by imposing stipulations such as demanding weekly attendance at their head office or paying 50 per cent commission on order and the balance when the customer pays. This can be very demotivating especially to the more experienced salespeople.

Case study

One company which used commission only salespeople to sell its service to the retail trade demanded that every representative attend the head office each Monday at 8.30am. Each person then had to stand up and read out their previous week's sales figures and with few exceptions were then roundly criticised in public by the sales manager. Naturally such humiliation was too much for the majority and, not surprisingly, the staff turnover was high.

The best way to control the activities of independent salespeople is to discuss them on a one-to-one basis preferably on neutral territory, such as a hotel reception area. This also helps the salesperson to feel respected by their manager.

If it is not possible to arrange regular meetings, speak to them on the telephone each week. Daily contact can be too pressurising for many.

Motivating

Naturally, being self-employed, they are motivated by money to a large extent. If they don't sell they don't earn. Nevertheless this does not mean they have no other needs. Show respect for their experience by asking for their ideas and opinions. Offer help and guidance, do not impose it. Keep paperwork to a minimum; the less you require the more likely you are to get it. Offer individual incentives rather than team ones. Salespeople working on commission are less likely to be team players than those employed. Make sure that the systems and environment are as motivating as possible. Nothing demotivates a commission only salesperson more than late payment of their earnings.

Case study

A company selling energy saving services to industry had six commission only representatives. The sales manager met up with each one in a hotel every two weeks. They would discuss sales figures, prospective customers, product developments and company news. The manager would list any problems or complaints that could not be dealt with on the spot. As soon as answers were available they would be communicated to the salesperson concerned. Once every quarter, the manager would arrange a team meeting, again in a hotel. These meetings would include a short training session and the attendance of a company director who would give a brief talk on the company's progress. Whilst retaining their independence, the salespeople felt valuable and part of the company.

To get the best from commission only sales representatives, you should manage them as you would any other sales force. It can help, when it comes to control, if you pay them a small retainer to help cover their expenses. Remember to consider the following points:

- always pay commissions promptly and in full
- provide and pay for adequate training
- offer achievable incentives
- encourage suggestions, ideas and opinions
- never impose unacceptable restrictions or penalties
- show respect by treating them as intelligent, experienced individuals
- encourage regular communication.

MANAGING AGENTS

Agents are self-employed individuals who 'represent' a firm's products and sell to regular customers and new prospects. Many agents carry the product lines of three or four non-competitive companies.

As most agents are experienced salespeople, they will need little in the way of control or motivation from the companies that they represent. Their main requirements are for good competitively priced products, no hassle from the companies, and prompt payment of commission. A number of companies also pay their agents a small monthly retainer of £150-£200, in an attempt to retain their loyalty. Because they are free agents, the best way to manage such people is to:

- Hold monthly, one-to-one meetings to exchange ideas and information.
- Give them ready telephone access to you and the company.
- Provide product support as required by them.

MANAGING A CONTRACT SALES FORCE

A contract sales force, sometimes known as commandos or mercenaries, is a sales team employed by a company which hires out their services to other firms. This happens for example when a company decides to carry out a specific sales campaign over say three or six months, but lacks sufficient salespeople to cover the area quickly. Contract sales forces are most commonly used in the fast-moving consumer goods area such as confectionery, foodstuffs, detergents and so on.

Many years ago I became involved in such an operation. An overseas fruit marketing board wished to promote sales of their country's oranges and grapefruits. They engaged a contract sales force to visit every greengrocery outlet in specific towns and cities to coincide with a major TV and press advertising campaign, to sell their products to and through the retailers. The whole exercise, which proved to be most successful, took six weeks and involved over 100 salespeople.

Small businesses which cannot afford to employ their own sales staff may also use contract salespeople on a short or a long term basis to promote their products.

If you are the direct sales manager of such a team, it should be managed as any traditional sales force, using the principles discussed in this book. The salespeople will need regular product training to deal with each situation. However, it is rare for such a sales force to be used to sell products of a highly technical or complex nature. If you are employing a contract sales force, it is highly unlikely that you will be able to exercise any direct influence on its individual members. Your contact will be their sales manager, with whom you should maintain regular contact to exchange information.

MANAGING A TELE-SALES TEAM

These are salespeople who are based in an office and who use the telephone as their main selling tool. The work can take the form of

- contacting regular customers to obtain their orders, or
- telephoning prospects to persuade them to buy the company's products or services.

Most often it is a combination of both.

Because tele-salespeople work in very close proximity to each other, the moods and attitudes of one person can affect the others very quickly. Therefore one of the main tasks of the sales manager is to promote and maintain a positive attitude within the team. Quite naturally, if a salesperson receives a series of rejections from prospects, he or she can become very despondent. The manager must ensure, through the right training, that these feelings are not transmitted to the rest of the team. On the other hand, when someone has been particularly successful, why not let everyone know? Whenever you go into a tele-sales office where the staff are highly motivated, you will find a definite buzz about the place.

Example: selling trade advertising

A publishing company produced a range of trade journals and employed several tele-sales teams to sell advertising space. Each team was responsible for a certain number of journals. Every salesperson had a group of regular clients with whom they had to maintain regular contact. In addition they were expected to sell to firms who did not advertise, or who only did so occasionally. The targets were set by the sales director. It was an interesting experience to visit the different sales teams. Some were buoyant, highly motivated and successful. In other cases, as you entered their office you could cut the atmosphere with a knife, and they really struggled to reach target. In every instance this was down to the way in which they were managed, particularly how they were motivated, and how the targets were presented to them.

Some key management techniques

Managing a tele-sales team is similar to managing any other salaried sales team but the following are of particular importance:

- Encourage and foster a close team spirit.

- Encourage each salesperson to help and support his or her colleagues.

- Provide small incentives, such as a bottle of wine or a box of chocolates, to encourage success.

- Remember to praise effort as well as success.

- Allow each person to take regular, short breaks. Tele-sales requires a great deal of concentration.

- Always involve the team in decisions which will affect them directly.

- Encourage ideas and suggestions from the team.

- Give help and support as required, but do not appear to be checking up on them.

Managing a tele-canvassing team

Strictly speaking this is not a sales team. Its purpose is principally to obtain appointments for the sales team. This is particularly common where commission-only salespeople are used to sell directly to the public. Tele-canvass teams are also used to gain market research information.

These teams should be managed in the same manner as a tele-sales force.

MANAGING RETAIL SALES STAFF

In most cases, the store, shop or department manager is responsible for these people. The manager should manage his/her retail salespeople as one would any salaried sales team. The main difference is that the manager and the team are in close proximity to one another, so good interpersonal skills are particularly important for the manager.

A number of large chain stores employ regional sales managers who are responsible for training the salespeople in sales and merchandising techniques.

CHOOSING THE RIGHT SALES TEAM FOR YOUR COMPANY

You may be in the enviable position of being appointed sales manager for a company that does not have a sales force. In this case you will have the luxury of deciding on the type of sales team most appropriate for your company and its products or services.

To help you in your decision, here are a few points to consider.

Choosing salaried salespeople

This includes salespeople who are paid salaries plus commission and/or bonuses. They are particularly useful where the product is of a technical nature and the salespeople will be expected to provide customers with technical advice; similarly where sales require several visits before an order can be secured, *eg* computer systems. Salaried sales teams are also employed where regular visits are made to customers to obtain orders, *eg* food, drink, confectionery.

Pros
- More control and direction over the salespeople.
- Easier to engender a team spirit.

- Greater loyalty by the sales team to you and the company.

Cons

- Expensive. You must pay salaries, provide cars and so on, regardless of value of sales generated.
- Normally require one month's notice of dismissal.
- More 'sales support' needed, which can be costly.

Choosing commission only sales people

Ideal where a large sales force is needed to sell non-technical products or services.

Pros

- Inexpensive. The only outgoing is commission which is based on sales revenue.
- If properly recruited, they will be experienced salespeople.

Cons

- Difficult to control and direct.
- Salespeople can leave without notice.
- Little or no company loyalty.

Choosing sales agents

Suitable where the company is too small to employ salespeople. Also ideal where the market is widespread or remote and it is not viable to employ a salesperson. Agents are often used to service overseas markets.

Pros

- Inexpensive, as with commission only.
- Will have experience and contacts in the market.
- Normally agents are mature business people.

Cons

- Difficult to control and direct.
- Will also be selling other companies' products or services.
- Large turnover, resulting in higher recruitment costs.

Choosing contract sales staff

Used by companies which cannot justify employing their own salespeople. Also employed for specific, short-term sales campaigns.

Pros
- Costs can be budgeted.
- Usually experienced salespeople.

Cons
- No direct control possible.
- Unsuitable where detailed product knowledge is required.

Choosing tele-sales staff

Very suitable for obtaining regular orders from customers for such products as food, drink and other fast moving goods. Useful for maintaining contact with past and geographically remote customers.

Pros
- Less expensive than a 'field' sales team.
- Easier to control, direct and motivate.

Cons
- Limitations of the telephone.
- Not suitable for technical or complex products.

QUESTIONS AND ANSWERS

Can I insist that my commission only salespeople work exclusively for my company?

No. These people are normally self-employed and such a restriction on their working activities is illegal.

How can I ensure that my commission only salespeople do not sell competitive products?

It is quite in order to ask them to sign an agreement prohibiting them from selling competitive products or services whilst working for you and for up to two years after leaving your company.

What is an Agency Agreement?

This is a written agreement between the company and the agent setting out such details as: commission payment terms, product range, geographical area, administration. It is signed by both parties with a copy for each.

Do I have to pay VAT to my agents and commission only salespeople?

Yes, if they are individually registered for VAT. It is paid on the commission earned.

EXERCISES

1. Given *carte blanche*, what changes would you make regarding the type of sales team used by your company, and why?

2. One of your commission only salesmen is not following up the leads generated by the tele-canvassing department. How would you overcome this problem?

3. You wish to appoint an agent for the north of Scotland to sell your company's product range. What specific experience would you seek from applicants for this agency?

Some Final Thoughts

- When sales are difficult to obtain and the pressure is on, your team will need more help and motivation from you.

- Time spent training well is time well spent.

- Unachievable targets are unlikely to be achieved.

- Sales meetings should be worth while attending.

- Delegate to develop your team.

- Use the strengths of each and every member of your team.

- Keep paperwork to a minimum.

- Field visits should be motivating.

- Criticise the action, not the person.

- Praise is inexpensive to give but valuable to receive.

- Involve your team in forecasts and budgets.

- Your team should work with you, not for you.

- You don't have to be the best salesperson in your team, just the best manager.

- Remember you are a manager, so manage.

Appendix:
Is your behaviour appropriate?

SELF ASSESSMENT

The way in which people behave towards you will largely depend upon how you behave towards them. Much of this behaviour is verbal. As a sales manager, you will need to use the appropriate behaviours towards your staff, colleagues and managers to gain their cooperation and at the same time to establish your position.

The following assessment, if answered honestly, will enable you to discover your usual way of behaving. There follows an explanation of the advantages and disadvantages of the four main behavioural types.

To complete the inventory, read each statement and circle the number of the response that is most characteristic of your behaviour, as you perceive it. Evaluate your behaviour as it is today, not as it once was, not as you would like it to be but, as it actually is.

You have a choice of circling numbers 0–4; each one means:

0 = completely uncharacteristic, meaning, I never do this (except on rare occasions).

1 = Quite uncharacteristic, meaning I usually do not do this.

2 = Somewhat characteristic, meaning I do this sometimes.

3 = Quite characteristic, meaning I usually do this.

4 = Completely characteristic, meaning I always do this (except on rare occasions).

QUESTIONNAIRE

1. I believe I have the right to say 'NO' to others without feeling guilty.　　0 1 2 3 4

2. I feel superior to most people I work with.　　0 1 2 3 4

3. When I am angry, I keep my feelings to myself. 0 1 2 3 4

4. If my rights are violated, I find a subtle but sure 0 1 2 3 4
   way to get even.

5. I do not have difficulty in maintaining eye contact 0 1 2 3 4
   with others.

6. I let people know when I disagree with them. 0 1 2 3 4

7. When others annoy me, I say nothing but show 0 1 2 3 4
   my displeasure through my body language.

8. I like to control others with behind the scenes 0 1 2 3 4
   manoeuvres.

9. I'm afraid to admit that I don't know how to do 0 1 2 3 4
   something I am expected to learn.

10. When people don't keep their commitment, I am 0 1 2 3 4
    reluctant to tell them I am upset.

11. I consider myself a demanding person. 0 1 2 3 4

12. If others are rude, I am rude back. 0 1 2 3 4

13. I express anger to others at the time it is 0 1 2 3 4
    appropriate to do so.

14. If I have something to say that I think is 0 1 2 3 4
    important, I will interrupt a conversation.

15. I feel uncomfortable when someone compliments 0 1 2 3 4
    my work.

16. When people take advantage of me I silently 0 1 2 3 4
    even the score.

17. I don't mind asking for help when I need it. 0 1 2 3 4

18. I don't hesitate to accuse others when I believe 0 1 2 3 4
    I have solid grounds for my suspicions.

19. I try to behave in ways that will make me 0 1 2 3 4
    popular with others.

20. I don't disagree with others openly, but they 0 1 2 3 4
    always seem to know when I'm put out with them.

21. If I don't agree with my boss, I may find a way to 0 1 2 3 4
    quietly drag my feet on projects he/she wants done.

22. I am able to be honest and open about my needs 0 1 2 3 4
    without feeling guilty.

23. I use sarcasm to make points. 0 1 2 3 4

24. I feel that I must comply with other people's 0 1 2 3 4
    requests.

25. I express my anger through various characteristic 0 1 2 3 4
    facial expressions.

26. I tend to be uncomfortable in unfamiliar 0 1 2 3 4
    surroundings.

27. I point my finger or use other gestures to add 0 1 2 3 4
    emphasis to my assertions.

28. I am able to express my feelings honestly and 0 1 2 3 4
    and directly.

29. If I don't like a person, I find a round-about 0 1 2 3 4
    means of letting him/her know.

30. I feel guilty when I have to ask others to do 0 1 2 3 4
    their share.

31. I like to be in control of every situation. 0 1 2 3 4

32. I accord others the same rights I accord myself. 0 1 2 3 4

33. When I am angry with someone, I give him/her 0 1 2 3 4
    the silent treatment.

34. When someone gets angry with me, I get angry 0 1 2 3 4
    in return.

35. I do favours for others even when I would prefer 0 1 2 3 4
    not to do them.

36. I prefer indirect ways of controlling others. 0 1 2 3 4

37. I don't like to say things directly that might 0 1 2 3 4
    hurt people's feelings.

38. I make decisions when I have a reasonable 0 1 2 3 4
    amount of information even though I may
    be wrong.

39. I believe you must show others your strength 0 1 2 3 4
    regardless of the situation if you want to
    command respect.

40. I am not as concerned about winning as I am   0 1 2 3 4
    concerned about negotiating reasonable
    arguments and relationships with others.

SCORING THE INVENTORY

To understand your score you first need to transfer the points assigned to the 40 items in the inventory to the rearranged lists below. Add the points in each column for total column scores. The items have been grouped under the four items described: Assertive, Passive, Concealed Aggressive and, Openly Aggressive.

Assertive	*Passive*	*Concealed Aggressive*	*Openly Aggressive*
1 --------	3 --------	4 -------	2 --------
5 --------	9 --------	7 -------	11 -------
6 --------	10 -------	8 -------	12 -------
13 -------	15 -------	16 ------	14 -------
17 -------	19 -------	20 ------	18 -------
22 -------	24 -------	21 ------	23 -------
28 -------	26 -------	25 ------	27 -------
32 -------	30 -------	29 ------	31 -------
38 -------	35 -------	33 ------	34 -------
40 -------	37 -------	36 ------	39 -------
Totals [ ]	[ ]	[ ]	[ ]

EXPLANATION

Openly aggressive behaviour

This may be defined as domineering, pushy, self-centred and self-enhancing. It results when a person gives little consideration to the thoughts and feelings of others. People who are openly aggressive in the extreme may be abusive, threatening and authoritarian. They tend to speak loudly using threatening words and tone. Their non-verbal behaviour may take the form of glaring, finger pointing and other angry movements.

Such behaviour may achieve results in the short term. However, people will be reluctant to discuss problems or personal matters with those who constantly use this behaviour.

Concealed aggressive behaviour

This is a more subtle way of conveying his/her reactions and feelings without consideration of others. This behaviour manifests itself in such ways as ignoring other people and their ideas and suggestions; making sarcastic remarks and criticising people behind their backs.

This behaviour is more dangerous than open aggression as others do not know where they stand with the user of concealed aggression.

Passive behaviour

The passive individual tends to ignore his/her own needs and feelings in an attempt to satisfy the needs and feelings of others. As a result such people often experience feelings of low esteem, frustration and withdrawal. Passive behaviour is inhibited and avoids conflict, however, such people are usually 'put upon' because they are unable to say No. Managers who use this behaviour normally end up 'doing' instead of 'managing'.

Assertive behaviour

This is open and respectful of the rights of others whilst recognising one's own rights at the same time. Assertive people are able to communicate their thoughts and feelings in ways that do not violate the rights of others.

Assertiveness can be described as:

- An active and initiating rather than a reactive behaviour.
- Caring, emphasising the positive nature of self and others.
- A non-judgemental attitude.
- Communicating needs, dislikes and feelings in a clear, direct manner without threatening or attacking others.
- Standing up for one's rights without denying the rights of others.

As assertive behaviour is defined as the most effective type for communication with others, scores in the 29 – 40 range would be most desirable.

Suggested Answers to Exercises

Chapter 1

3. Arrange a meeting with your managing director to define and agree your responsibilities. Explain the effect his interventions are having on the sales team.

Chapter 2

2. • The previous year's actual sales revenue figures by customer type and product for the team and each salesperson.
   • Known future events such as exhibitions, promotions and new product launches.
   • Competitive activity.

3. Everyone needs standards to which to aspire. Behavioural standards are particularly important for salespeople as they are representing the company to the outside world. Therefore the right appearance and clean cars and equipment reflect well upon the company.

Chapter 3

3. It is essential to talk with Mike as soon as possible. Don't assume reasons for the changes. He may need a challenge or development towards management.

Chapter 4

3. (a) Hard – Alex Taylor is highly task orientated.
   (b) (i)   Kept salesmen waiting in his office.
       (ii) 'Grimshaws is a very different kettle of fish.'
       (iii) 'You will have to work to earn your money.'
       (iv) Sales meetings at 5.30pm on Fridays.
       (v)   No excuses for non-attendance.
       (vi) 'Training?...pick it up as you go along.'
   (c) Very low – probably very demotivated.
   (d) Demotivated staff – high staff turnover. Discuss with Alex the benefits to him of changing his style; suggest training.
   (e) If the situation is allowed to continue, sales revenue is likely

to suffer. Taylor's attitude could affect other departments; recruitment costs will rise.

Chapter 5

2. If he is the ideal candidate for the job, ensure that he understands and accepts your position and offer him the job.

Chapter 6

3. Arrange a meeting with all of your team. Explain how you intend to undertake field visits and emphasise the importance and benefits to the team. Then go ahead with your proposals.

Chapter 7

3. First, question your behaviour towards him. Change his behaviour by changing yours. Ask for his suggestions, encourage his participation and give him genuine praise as appropriate.

Chapter 8

2. Advantages include:
   - it gives the meeting meaning and importance
   - avoids interruptions
   - if the hotel is centrally sited, no one is penalised by longer journeys than others
   - easier to control the meeting
   - refreshments easily available.

   Disadvantages include:
   - cost of room hire and refreshments
   - you must ensure you have all necessary information and documents with you.

3. Arrange to meet your sales director. Ask his reasons for wanting weekly meetings. Explain your purpose for holding sales meetings. Emphasis the cost to the company in lost sales and travel by taking the team away from their territories.

Chapter 9

2. Plot the past sales volumes for Hoppits and Toppits on separate graphs. Extrapolate the 'lines of best fit' to cover years 7, 8 and 9. Adjust the estimated volumes of Hoppits for these years by 10k for the lost business and similarly adjust the volume of Toppits by 5 per cent. Increase all sales volumes to account for the new salesperson. As this person will need time to become fully effective, appropriate increases would be 10 per cent for year 7; 15 per cent for year 8 and 20 per cent for year 9. If you

believe that the new Italian imports will affect your market share, reduce the volume of Hoppits by a small percentage. Multiply the resulting sales volumes by the new prices to obtain the annual sales revenue forecasts.

Chapter 10

2. Differences between direct and exhibition selling:

Direct selling	Exhibition selling
The willingness to speak to you has already been established.	You have to persuade people to stop and talk to you.
The name of the company and contact are known.	You will need to discover the visitor's name, company and position.
You decide your objectives before the interview.	You need to discover your objectives during the interview.
Background information is already available.	Little or no information available.
You can plan sufficient time for the interview.	Interviews need to be short so as not to miss other prospects.
The product may be too large to demonstrate on customers premises.	Product available for demonstration on the stand.
Company backing not visible.	Company backing can be seen and proved.
Technical advice may not be readily available.	Other company personnel in attendance.

3. Time-wasters can be discouraged by asking direct, specific questions about their needs, purchasing intentions and so on. Display your literature in a position which makes poeople come on to your stand to obtain it. Paper collectors will be less likely to venture on to your stand.

Chapter 12

2. Arrange to meet the person concerned, preferably on neutral territory. Ask if there is any specific reason for not following up the leads and if there are any problems such as travelling, difficulties in selling the product or other commitments.

Your next move will depend upon his answers. You may suggest more training or other assistance, or simply terminate the agreement.

4. Home location; experience of selling similar products; market knowledge of the area; existing commitments with other companies; how long he has been a freelance agent.

Glossary

Advertising – method by which an organisation attempts to make the public aware of its products and services.

Agents – self-employed people who sell the products/services of one or more companies in return for commission-based payment.

Below the line – term given to all forms of promotion except advertising ('above-the-line').

Break even point – the point where sales revenue equals cost. Above this the company begins to make a profit.

Budget – estimate of expenditure and income over a given period or for a specific project.

Commission – money paid to salespeople based upon their sales volume.

Controlled circulation (cc) – journal sent free to selected people.

CV – curriculum vitae ('course of life'), a summary of a person's education and career background.

Delegation – the process of transferring tasks or projects to other people.

Direct mail – means of promotion which involves sending literature and/or samples to customers and prospects.

Direct sales – sales made to the user directly from the manufacturer or agency.

Employee profile – qualities required of candidates for a job vacancy.

Extrapolate – to extend from existing data, for example the 'line of best fit' on a sale forecast graph.

Field sales – selling directly to the customer on a face-to-face basis.

Field visits – when a sales manager accompanies a sales representative on visits to customers and prospects with the object of developing that representative.

FMCG – Fast Moving Consumer Goods such as food, drink and other consumable products.

Forecast – estimate for future sales revenue or volume based upon past performance and existing economic and market conditions.

Induction – initial training, for example as given to a new salesperson.

Job description – document detailing the duties, responsibilities and parameters of a job.

Leadership style – method a manager adopts to manager his/her resources.

Line management – managers below board level.

Line of best fit – straight line on a graph of past sales performance which best fits the plotted points.

Mail shot – another term for direct mail.

Management – getting things done through others.

Marketing – in the context of this book it refers to sales support activities such as market research and promotion.

Market research – means by which a company obtains external views and opinions of its products, services, customer service and so on.

Mentor – person assigned to help others.

Merchandising – arranging displays of products in a retail outlet, designed to attract customers; may also refer to point of sale promotions.

Newstrade – journals purchased through retail outlets.

OTE – on target earnings. Commission received when achieving set targets.

Paperwork – collective term for reports that a sales executive is obliged to complete on a regular basis.

Pareto's Rule – 80 per cent of a company's sales revenue is generated by 20 per cent of its customers.

People orientated – leadership style where the manager concentrates on ensuring that his/her staff are satisfied; the task takes second place.

Point of sale – position in a retail outlet where a company's goods are displayed and promoted.

Promotion – methods used by companies to increase sales of its goods and services.

Prospects – individuals and organisations who are potential customers.

Representative – one who represents a company in a sales capacity.

Retail outlet – shops, stores and so on.

Retail sales – sales made through retail outlets.

Retainer – a sum of money paid to agents and commission only salespeople, often on a monthly basis, to retain their loyalty.

Sales revenue – money received or expected in return for goods and services sold.

Sales volume – quantity of goods sold or targeted.

Target – amount of sales revenue or volume which each salesperson is expected to generate over a given period of time.

Task orientated – leadership style whereby the manager concentrates on achieving the task objectives to the exclusion of the welfare of the staff.

Tele-can – telephone canvassing; contacting prospects by telephone to obtain appointments for sales representatives; also used to gain market information.

Tele-sales – contacting customers and prospects by telephone with the objective of obtaining orders.

Territory – geographically defined sales area.

Variance – difference between budgeted expenditure and income and the actual amounts spent and received.

Useful Addresses

PROFESSIONAL BODIES

Advertising Association, 15 Wilton Road, London SW1V 1LT. Tel: (0171) 828 2771.

Association of Conference Executives, Riverside House, High Street, Huntingdon, Cambridgeshire PE18 6SG. Tel: (01480) 457595. Fax: (01480) 411341.

Chartered Institute of Marketing, Moor Hall, Cookham, Berkshire SL6 9QH. Tel: (01628) 524922. Fax: (01628) 522104. The leading professional body in the UK for marketing and sales executives. Training services are provided by a division of the Institute, CIM Marketing Training.

Communications, Advertising & Marketing Foundation, Abford House, 15 Wilton Road, London SW1V 1NJ. Tel: (0171) 828 7506. Fax: (0171) 936 5140.

Industrial Marketing Research Association, 11 Bird Street, Lichfield, Staffordshire WS13 6PW. Tel: (01543) 263448. Fax: (01543) 250929.

Institute of Export, 64 Clifton Street, London EC2A 4HB. Tel: (0171) 247 9812.

Institute of Personnel Management, IPM House, Camp Road, Wimbledon, London SW19 4UX. Tel: (0181) 946 9100.

Institute of Practitioners in Advertising, 44 Belgrave Square, London SW1X 8QR. Tel: (0171) 235 7020.

Institute of Public Relations, 15 Northburgh Street, London EC1V 0AH. Tel: (0171) 253 5151.

Institute of Sales & Marketing Management, 31 Upper George Street, Luton, Bedfordshire LU1 2RD. Tel: (01582) 411130. Fax: (01582) 453640.

Furher Reading

GENERAL

How To Be An Even Better Manager, Michael Armstrong (Kogan Page, 1988)
Managing Individual Performance, Kieran Baldwin (How To Books, 1999)
Managing Performance Reviews, Nigel Hunt (How To Books, 1999)
Managing Through People, John Humphries (How To Books, 1998)
The Management Handbook, Arthur Young (Sphere Books, 1986)
Organising Effective Training, James Chalmers (How To Books, 1996)
First Time Manager, Joan Iaconetti & Patrick O'Hara (MacMillan, 1985)

COMMUNICATION SKILLS IN BUSINESS

Mastering Business English, Michael Bennie (How To Books, 1998)
Mastering Public Speaking, Ann Nicholls (How To Books, 1998)
Publish a Newsletter, Graham Jones (How To Books, 1995)
Writing a Press Release, Peter Bartram (How To Books, 1999)
Writing a Report, John Bowden (How To Books, 1997)

FINANCE

Accounting & Finance for Business Students, Mike Bendry, Roger Hussey and Colston West (DP Publications, 1989)

INNOVATION

Master Thinkers Handbook, Edward de Bono (Penguin, 1985)
101 Ways To Generate Great Ideas, Timothy R V Foster (Kogan Page, 1992)

PROMOTIONS

Advertising, Frank Jefkins (Butterworth-Heinemann, 1991)
Do-It-Yourself Marketing Research, George Edward Brean (McGraw Hill, 1977)
How to Do Your Own Advertising, Michael Bennie (How To Books, 1995)

RECRUITMENT

How to Employ and Manage Staff, Wendy Wyatt (How To Books, 1995)
Recruiting for Results, Steve Kneeland (How To Books, 1999)

TEAMS AND LEADERSHIP

Effective Problem-Solving, Steve Kneeland (How To Books, 1999)
Managing Successful Teams, John Humphries (How To Books, 1998)
Not Bosses But Leaders, John Adair (Kogan Page, 1981)
Teamwork, Vincent Nolan (Sphere, 1987)

Index